W9-DBF-028

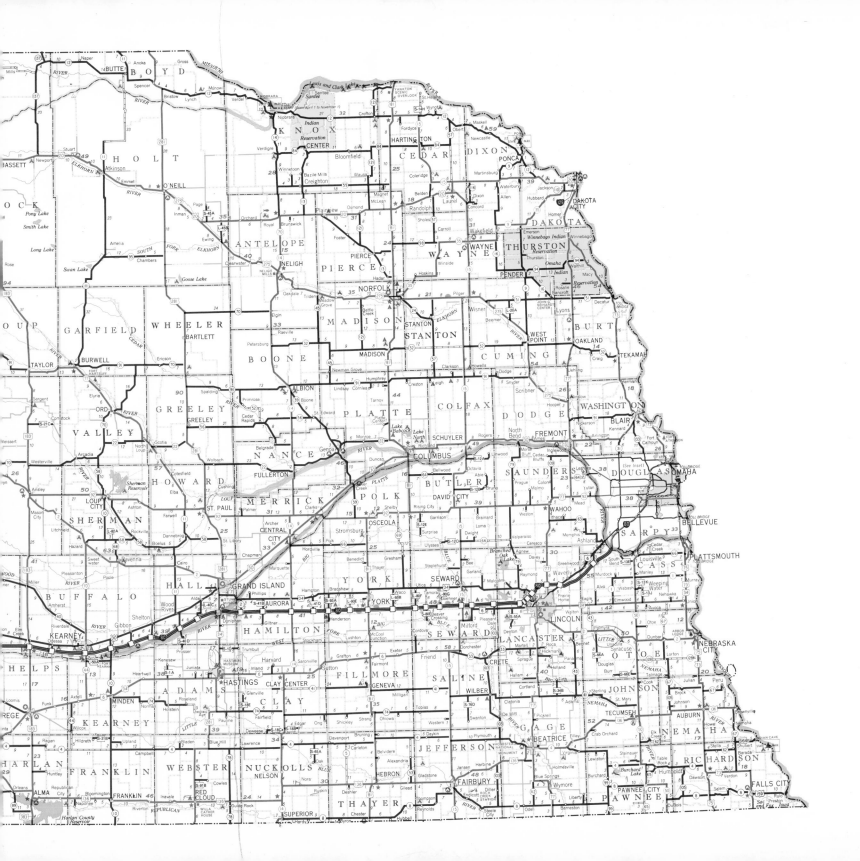

Climatic Atlas of Nebraska

Climatic Atlas of Nebraska

Project Director
Merlin P. Lawson

Contributing Authors
Merlin P. Lawson
Kenneth F. Dewey
Ralph E. Neild

Cartographer
John D. Magill

University of Nebraska Press • Lincoln and London

Research Assistants
GARY LISTER
SHAIL AGRAWAL

Publishers on the Plains
UNP

Copyright © 1977 by the University of Nebraska
Press
All rights reserved
Manufactured in the United States of America

Library of Congress Cataloging in Publication Data
Lawson, Merlin P   1941–
   Climatic atlas of Nebraska.
   "Appendix: State and Federal climatological publi-
cations": p. 87
   1. Nebraska—Climate.   I.   Dewey, Kenneth
Frederic, 1947–   joint author.   II.   Neild,
Ralph E., 1924–   joint author.   III.   Title.
QC984.N2L38   551.6'9'782   77–6643
ISBN 0–8032–0924–X

Prepared at the Laboratory for Cartographic Sciences,
Department of Geography, University of Nebraska–
Lincoln.

The publication of this atlas was assisted by a grant
from the Nebraska American Revolution Bicentennial
Commission.

Cover photograph reproduced by courtesy of the Nebraska Game and Parks Commission.

All color photos were provided by the Nebraska
Game and Parks Commission.

CONTENTS

LIST OF MAPS, GRAPHS, AND TABLES   vii

FOREWORD   xi
James H. Zumberge, Former Chancellor, University
of Nebraska–Lincoln

PREFACE   xiii
Merlin P. Lawson, Department of Geography,
University of Nebraska–Lincoln

1. INTRODUCTION   1

Nebraska's Climatic Controls   2
Merlin P. Lawson

Nebraska's Weather Stations   7
Kenneth F. Dewey, Department of Geography,
University of Nebraska–Lincoln

2. TEMPERATURE   11

Cold Winters   12
Ralph E. Neild, Department of Horticulture, Univer-
sity of Nebraska–Lincoln

A Winter Discomfort Index   16
Merlin P. Lawson

Heating Degree Days   18
Ralph E. Neild

Hot Summers   20
Ralph E. Neild

Cooling Degree-Days   23
Ralph E. Neild

Livestock Stress   24
Ralph E. Neild

Sunshine   26
Ralph E. Neild

The Progression of Spring across Nebraska   28
Ralph E. Neild

The Freeze-Free Season   29
Ralph E. Neild

The Agroclimatic Calendar   35
Ralph E. Neild

3. ATMOSPHERIC HUMIDITY AND PRECIPITATION   37

Nebraska's Hydrologic Cycle   38
Kenneth F. Dewey

Humidity   42
Merlin P. Lawson

Annual, Monthly, and Growing Season Precipitation   42
Kenneth F. Dewey

Precipitation Extremes   46
Kenneth F. Dewey and Merlin P. Lawson

Thunderstorms, Lightning, and Hail   47
Merlin P. Lawson

117529

Climatic Aspects of Drought in Nebraska   52
Merlin P. Lawson

Snowfall   59
Kenneth F. Dewey

Blizzards   64
Merlin P. Lawson

4. **WIND**   71

Wind Speed and Prevailing Direction   72
Kenneth F. Dewey

Shelterbelts: Modifying Nebraska's Microclimate   74
Merlin P. Lawson

Tornadoes: The Earth's Most Violent Winds   75
Merlin P. Lawson

5. **OUR CHANGING CLIMATE**   81

Urban-Rural Contrast in Weather and Climate   82
Kenneth F. Dewey

Climatic Fluctuation   84
Merlin P. Lawson

APPENDIX: STATE AND FEDERAL CLIMATOLOGICAL PUBLICATIONS   87
Merlin P. Lawson

MAPS, GRAPHS, AND TABLES

1. *Introduction*

Nebraska's Climatic Controls
Table   1 Length of Daylight at Grand Island   3
Figure   1 Monthly Extremes and Average Temperatures, 1941–70   3
Figure   2 Distribution of Precipitation, 1941–70   6

Nebraska Weather Stations
Figure   3 Nebraska Weather Stations   8

2. *Temperature*

Cold Winters
Figure   4 Mean Monthly Temperatures, October–March, 1941–70   12
Figure   5 Mean Annual Number of Days with Freezing Temperatures   13
Figure   6 Mean Annual Number of Days with Low Temperatures   13
Figure   7 Mean Annual Number of Days with Excessively Cold Temperatures   14
Figure   8 Longest Record of Consecutive Daily Temperatures below 10° F.   14
Figure   9 Longest Record of Consecutive Daily Temperatures below 0° F.   15
Figure 10 Longest Record of Consecutive Daily Temperatures below −5° F.   15
Figure 11 Longest Record of Consecutive Daily Temperatures below −10° F.   15

A Winter Discomfort Index
Table   2 Wind Chill Index   16

Heating Degree-Days
Figure 12 Mean Date of First Indoor Heating   18
Figure 13 Mean Annual Heating Degree-Days   18
Figure 14 Mean Daily Heating Degree-Days, January   19

Hot Summers
Figure 15 Mean Monthly Temperatures, April–September, 1941–70   20
Figure 16 Mean Annual Number of Days with High Temperatures   21
Figure 17 Longest Record of Consecutive Daily Temperatures above 90° F.   21
Figure 18 Longest Record of Consecutive Daily Temperatures above 94° F.   22
Figure 19 Longest Record of Consecutive Daily Temperatures above 100° F.   22
Figure 20 Longest Record of Consecutive Daily Temperatures above 104° F.   22

Cooling Degree-Days
Figure 21 Mean Annual Cooling Degree-Days   23
Figure 22 Mean Date of First Indoor Cooling   24
Figure 23 Mean Daily Cooling Degree-Days, July   24

Livestock Stress
Figure 24 Mean Annual Number of High-Temperature Stress Days for Cattle   25
Table   3 Average Dates and Duration of Temperatures above 80° F. at Selected Locations   25

Sunshine
    Figure 25 Mean Monthly Sunshine   26

The Progression of Spring across Nebraska
    Figure 26 Mean Daily Spring Temperatures   28

The Freeze-Free Season
    Figure 27 Mean Date of Last Spring Freeze   29
    Figure 28 Mean Annual Freeze-Free Season   30
    Figure 29 Mean Date of First Autumn Freeze   30
    Figure 30 Probability of Spring Freeze, April 1   31
    Figure 31 Probability of Spring Freeze, April 15   31
    Figure 32 Probability of Spring Freeze, May 1   32
    Figure 33 Probability of Spring Freeze, May 15   32
    Figure 34 Probability of Autumn Freeze, September 1   33
    Figure 35 Probability of Autumn Freeze, September 15   33
    Figure 36 Probability of Autumn Freeze, October 1   34
    Figure 37 Probability of Autumn Freeze, October 15   34

The Agroclimatic Calendar
    Graph 1 Planting and Harvest Times for Various Crops   35
    Table   4 Base Temperatures and Growing Degree-Day Requirements for Various Crops   35
    Figure 38 Mean Annual Growing Degree-Days with Temperatures above 50° F.   36
    Figure 39 Mean Annual Growing Degree-Days with Temperatures above 40° F.   36

3.   *Atmospheric Moisture and Precipitation*

Nebraska's Hydrologic Cycle
    Figure 40 The Hydrologic Cycle   38
    Graph 2 The Local Water Budget   40

Humidity
    Graph 3 Mean Monthly Humidity   42

Annual, Monthly, and Growing Season Precipitation
    Figure 41 Mean Annual Precipitation, 1941–70   43
    Figure 42 Mean Monthly Precipitation, 1941–70   43
    Figure 43 Mean Growing Season Precipitation   45
    Figure 44 Number of Days with Precipitation of Half an Inch or More   45

Precipitation Extremes
    Figure 45 Average Annual Maximum 1-Hour Rainfall   46
    Figure 46 Average Annual Maximum 24-Hour Rainfall   46
    Figure 47 100-Year Maximum 1-Hour Rainfall   46

Thunderstorms, Lightning, and Hail
    Figure 48 Mean Annual Number of Days with Thunderstorms   47
    Figure 49 Diagram of a Hail-Producing Thunderstorm   50
    Figure 50 Mean Annual Number of Days with Hail   51

Climatic Aspects of Drought in Nebraska
    Figure 51 Fort Kearny Meteorological Journal   53
    Graph 4 Correspondence of Average Annual Precipitation and Solar Activity in Nebraska, 1850–1970   54
    Figure 52 Precipitation Variability   55
    Figure 53 Areas of Major Soil Damage   55
    Table   5 Growing Season Precipitation, 1974–76   57
    Figure 54 Percentage of Months with Drought, 1931–69   58
    Figure 55 Maximum Number of Consecutive Months with Drought and Extreme Drought, 1931–69   58

Snowfall
    Figure 56 Mean Annual Snowfall, 1930–60   60
    Figure 57 Mean Annual Number of Days with Snowfall of Half an Inch or More   60

Figure 58 Mean Date of First 1-Inch Snowfall   61
Figure 59 Mean Date of Last 1-Inch Snowfall   61
Figure 60 Average Depth of Snow, December 1   62
Figure 61 Average Depth of Snow, January 1   62
Figure 62 Average Depth of Snow, February 1   63
Figure 63 Average Depth of Snow, March 1   63

4.   *Wind*

Wind Speed and Prevailing Direction
Figure 64 Average Monthly Wind Speed and Pre-
                vailing Direction   72
Tornadoes: The Earth's Most Violent Winds
Figure 65 Conditions Favorable to Tornado For-
                mation in Nebraska   77
Graph   5 Monthly Frequency of Tornadoes in
                Nebraska, 1953–72   77
Figure 66 Mean Annual Tornado Frequency   79
Figure 67 Total Number of Reported Tornadoes
                by County, 1950–73   79

5.   *Our Changing Climate*

Urban-Rural Contrast in Weather and Climate
Table   6 Comparison of Urban Climate with
                Climate of Surrounding Countryside   82
Table   7 Monthly Temperature and Precipitation
                Normals for Lincoln, Downtown and
                Airport, 1941–70   83
Figure 68 The Effect of Urbanism on Climate   84

FOREWORD

The climate of the planet Earth is a fundamental element of man's environment. For centuries it has been a topic of social conversation, but more recently it has become a subject of intense scientific interest. Climatology, the study of the earth's climate, is an inexact science because those who are serious students of climate do not understand the interaction of all the factors which cause climatic variations in time and space. And because the complex factors that cause certain climatic patterns are not understood, predictions of the trend of future climates for the earth in general or for any given region in particular are beyond the reach of climatologists.

Prediction, however, is the goal of the climatologist. It is not only an intellectual goal but a very practical one. Imagine, for example, the advantage of knowing what Nebraska's climate will be twenty-five years hence. Just to know the length of the growing season would provide a tremendous advantage to the research effort in agriculture. Or knowing the severity of winters or summers many years in advance would allow for intelligent planning of energy requirements for heating and air conditioning. The knowledge of future rainfall and snowfall patterns would prove invaluable to the management of surface and groundwater supplies with respect to irrigation requirements as well as municipal and industrial water supplies. These are just a few examples of why it is important for man to know what the future climate will be for any given region.

Man's ability to predict climates is a long-term goal. The first step in achieving that goal is to describe the present and past climatic conditions of a particular region in the most precise detail possible. The next step is to determine what natural forces are responsible for the present climatic conditions. Climatology is thus a true natural science in that it involves the relationships of cause and effect. In this case, the effect is the climate, and the cause is the interaction of all the factors, such as solar heating of the atmosphere, its moisture content, the distribution of land and sea, and the like, that produce the climatic patterns of the earth.

This volume is concerned primarily with a description of Nebraska's climate based on data collected over a number of years. Data from one or even two or three years do not describe the climate of a region. Day-to-day records of temperature, precipitation, humidity, and the like describe the *weather* of an area, whereas the *climate* of an area is based on average weather records of many years. A climatic atlas therefore tells what the average weather has been during the period of record, and cannot be used as a precise indicator of what the weather will be tomorrow, next week, or next year.

This is not to say, however, that a climatic atlas is not useful to the planner. The average length of the growing season, the average date of the last killing frost, and the average precipitation of a region are valuable guidelines to those engaged in agricultural and other enterprises. But variations from averages are the rule rather than the exception, and one can therefore expect years with more or less rainfall than the average, longer or shorter growing seasons than average, and summer or winter temperatures that are hotter or colder than average.

The planning and preparation of this atlas is mainly the work of Dr. Merlin P. Lawson of the Department of Geography at the University of Nebraska–Lincoln. When I first suggested the idea to him, he accepted it with enthusiasm. The result is a thoroughly professional account of the climate of Nebraska.

To Dr. Merlin Lawson, therefore, I express my personal thanks for undertaking this important task that has culminated in a document of considerable importance to the people of Nebraska. This volume is one of the many ways in which the University of Nebraska provides useful information to citizens of the State. In a very real sense, this book is a dividend paid to the Nebraskans from the investment of their tax dollars in support of the University.

James H. Zumberge,
Chancellor
University of Nebraska–Lincoln, 1972–75

President
Southern Methodist University, 1975–

PREFACE

An integral part of any region's natural resource base is its climatic character. Nebraska's history demonstrates the immense importance of the role that climate has played in the settlement of the state and development of a predominantly agricultural economy. As energy supplies continue to become scarce and expensive, Nebraska's climate may take on added importance as we investigate the sun and wind as sources of energy.

We are not interested in weather and climate wholly as a natural resource, however. Weather is a constant and sometimes dominating force in the lives of everyone. We are intrigued by its variability, often delighted by its splendor, and occasionally terrified by its misbehavior. Individual weather events can be generalized into a statistical description of the climatic parameters of a place. The ability to comprehend the processes which control a region's climate not only have application in our economic lives but adds to our appreciation of Nebraska's climatic diversity.

The *Climatic Atlas of Nebraska* is written for the layman as well as the sophisticated researcher to explain the spatial patterns of climatic elements. Most atlases simply present a collection of maps without satisfying the reader's curiosity about cause-and-effect relationships. In addition to summarizing graphically the totality of weather events, we have provided explanations of weather occurrences.

This volume is one of a series of topical atlases designed to offer comprehensive coverage of geographical information and analysis. The project originated in a directive from former chancellor James H. Zumberge of the University of Nebraska–Lincoln establishing the Nebraska Atlas Project "to provide a geographical inventory of the state of Nebraska by incorporating descriptive maps and graphs with explanatory narrative."

In producing this volume, the Department of Geography has relied on the voluntary efforts of many institutions, agencies, and individuals. As director of the Nebraska Atlas Project, I am especially indebted to Professors Kenneth F. Dewey and Ralph E. Neild for their interpretative narratives. Their contribution to the project represents an overload to their normal academic commitments. My sincere gratitude is also extended to John D. Magill, chief cartographer for the project, whose expertise and imagination added immeasurably to the project. Much of the statistical information was made available through the cooperation of two Nebraska agencies. Dr. Mahendra Bansal of the Nebraska Natural Resources Commission provided many of the unpublished statistical summaries required for this atlas; and Richard Myers and Esther Culwell, formerly with the State Climatology Office of the National Weather Service, but now associated with the Conservation and Survey Division, University of Nebraska–Lincoln, supplied most of the published data sources.

I would like to express my sincere gratitude to the Nebraska American Revolution Bicentennial Commission for providing matching funds for the preparation of this volume. Their special recognition is greatly appreciated.

Finally, this volume is dedicated to the hundreds of volunteer weather observers of the past century who have given freely of their time to record Nebraska's weather.

MERLIN P. LAWSON
Director, Nebraska Atlas Project

1
Introduction

Nebraska's Climatic Controls
Nebraska's Weather Stations

The planet Earth is composed of three general environmental spheres: the solid crust of the earth, or lithosphere; the water surface, or hydrosphere; and the gaseous atmosphere. The ocean of air above the land and water surface is an integral component of the planet, the surface of which actually extends to the edge of the atmosphere. This atmospheric envelope makes life on the planet possible, for without its special properties the terrestrial earth would have a temperature of −4° F. (−20° C.), approximately 60° F. (33° C.) below the present average air temperature. This gaseous layer not only provides a mechanism for maintaining a life-supporting thermal balance, but aids in shielding organisms—including human life—from the harmful effects of solar ultraviolet radiation.

The complex of chemical and physical processes that effect the interaction of heat and moisture in the atmosphere is studied in great detail by atmospheric scientists. The day-to-day state of the atmosphere and the processes behind atmospheric changes are interpreted by meteorologists according to principles of atmospheric physics. Long-term patterns of atmospheric conditions, including heat, moisture, and air circulation, are comprehensively studied by climatologists. Thus, the sciences of meteorology and climatology have similar foundations, the latter encompassing the cumulative impact or expression of atmospheric elements and processes from place to place over a more extended period of time.

Our concern in this atlas is to illustrate climatological patterns throughout the state by describing weather elements over the long term. These elements consist primarily of solar radiation, duration of sunshine, temperature, humidity, evaporation, cloudiness, precipitation, barometric pressure, and winds. However, the climate of a region like Nebraska is more than a basic description of the variations in the amount, intensity, and distribution of certain observable elements. The occurrence of those elements must be explained and interpreted in terms of climatic controls and their influence on meteorological processes.

NEBRASKA'S CLIMATIC CONTROLS

Day-to-day weather processes which determine a region's climatic character are regulated by climatic controls such as latitude, elevation, the distribution of land and water, mountain barriers, persistent pressure centers with their resultant prevailing winds, air masses, and ocean circulation. These controls, acting in combination, produce the variations in climatic elements that distinguish patterns of climate over an extended period of time. By relating these controls to the weather patterns of Nebraska, we can derive a more comprehensive understanding of the state's climate. .

Latitude

The distribution of solar radiation, the source of 99.97 percent of the total energy available to the atmosphere, is determined primarily by the spherical shape of the earth. Only half of the earth's surface can receive solar beams at any given moment, and much of that radiation falls at a fairly oblique angle. The amount of energy available at a particular latitude depends primarily upon two factors: the angle at which the sun's noon rays strike the earth (intensity), and the length of the daily period of sunlight (duration).

When the sun's noonday rays are directly perpendicular to the earth, the area is receiving the maximum intensity of solar energy. This angle of incidence varies as a function of latitude and the seasons. In winter at high latitudes the angle of the sun at noon is relatively low. The effectiveness of solar radiation (insolation) is diminished because the oblique rays are spread over a greater surface, producing less heating per unit of area than perpendicular rays.

Illustrating this principle in Nebraska, the lowest angle of the winter's noon sun at Grand Island is about 26° above the horizon, resulting in a loss of 56 percent of the energy available to a perpendicular surface. Late in June, when the noon sun is 73° above the horizon, the solar intensity is only 5 percent less than its maximum potential. Thus, winter sunlight is much weaker than that of summer because of the angle at which the sunlight reaches the curved surface of the earth.

The duration of daylight, which ultimately affects the total possible insolation, also varies with latitude on a seasonal basis. The length of daylight ranges from a constant twelve hours at the equator to a maximum of twenty-four hours in the polar regions during the summer and a minimum of zero hours in winter. Again using Grand Island to illustrate the relationship (table 1), the longest summer day (June 21) in this central Nebraska city has approximately six hours more of daylight than the shortest winter day (December 21). Solar radiation during summer in Nebraska exceeds insolation at the equator because of the longer hours of daylight in the higher latitudes. The longer duration, coupled with the more perpendicular angle of the sun's rays, results in high summer temperatures, while chilling

Table 1. Length of Daylight at Grand Island

First of Month	Sunrise	Sunset	Hours and Minutes of Daylight
	(Central Standard Time)		
January	7:58	5:16	9:18
February	7:44	5:50	10:06
March	7:08	6:24	11:16
April	6:17	6:58	12:41
May	5:32	7:30	13:58
June	5:04	7:59	14:55
July	5:05	8:09	15:04
August	5:29	7:50	14:21
September	6:00	7:06	13:06
October	6:29	6:16	11:47
November	7:04	5:30	10:26
December	7:38	5:06	9:28

SOURCE: Nautical Almanac Office, U.S. Naval Observatory.

winter conditions are due to the lower angle of the sun and the considerably shorter period of insolation (fig. 1).

Elevation

In the lower portion of the atmosphere (below approximately 35,000 feet), temperature normally decreases with increasing elevation. This indicates that the lower atmosphere absorbs the terrestrial reradiation (the heat radiated back from the earth) more efficiently than thinner, dryer air aloft.

Although varying with time of day, season, and place, temperature normally declines approximately 3.5° F. with every 1,000 feet (or 6° C. per kilometer) of increased altitude. Since portions of Nebraska's Panhandle reach elevations of over

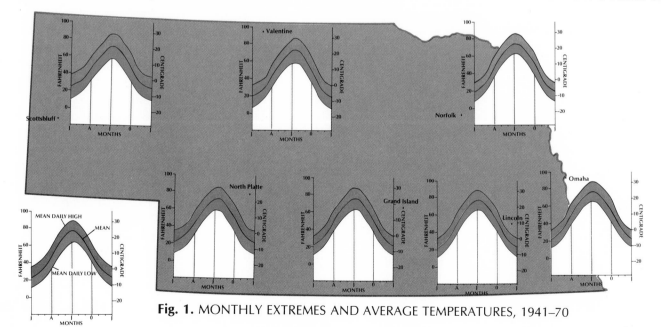

Fig. 1. MONTHLY EXTREMES AND AVERAGE TEMPERATURES, 1941–70

5,000 feet, one should expect cooler temperatures there than in the southeastern corner of the state, with elevations close to four-fifths of a mile lower. The growing season, or frost-free period, likewise decreases as elevation increases across the state.

Distribution of Land and Water

Nebraska's interior continental position is an important climatic control having an impact on numerous elements of weather or climate. If the earth's surface were composed of a uniform material (for instance, water) at a common elevation (sea level), the earth's temperature would vary primarily with latitude. The distribution of continents, however, disrupts this pattern because a land surface is capable of reaching higher temperatures than a water surface receiving the same amount of solar energy. Conversely, the land surface reradiates heat at a faster rate, thus cooling to a lower temperature in a given time period. The result is a more extreme range of temperatures over continents than over oceans on both a daily and seasonal basis. This contrast is even greater at latitudes similar to that of Nebraska and higher because land surfaces cannot store as much heat as ocean waters, which distribute it throughout a greater volume. During periods of net heat loss, cooled surface water sinks, to be replaced by less dense, warmer water, which rises from below. There is also a redistribution of heat by ocean currents, which predominantly carry it out of the tropical regions toward the poles. The slow release of transported and stored thermal energy prevents extremely low temperatures from occurring over bodies of water.

Nebraska's interior position, remote from any oceans or sizable lakes, results in a "continentality effect" which denotes a wide annual range of temperatures (fig. 1). The extremes of heat and cold as measured four feet above the ground are among the greatest in the contiguous states. For example, in 1974 Lincoln experienced a span of 138 degrees F. (76.7 degrees C.), ranging from 33° F. below zero (−36.1° C.) on January 12 to 105° F. (40.6° C.) on June 30. When one considers the divergence between normal summer and winter temperatures, this example may not be very impressive. Yet most weather stations in the state have recorded a range of over 100 degrees F. (55.6° C.) between maximum and minimum January temperatures alone!

Daily temperatures also reflect the effect of land surface heating and cooling rates. On clear, sunny days the maximum intensity of incoming radiation is greatest around noon. Temperature readings rise rapidly during the early morning hours following sunrise and continue to rise at a diminished rate until around two or three hours after the solar radiation maximum has been reached for the day. The daily march of temperatures is not reversed until terrestrial reradiation exceeds incoming solar radiation (i.e., until the earth loses more heat than it receives from the sun). Thus, daily maximum temperatures normally occur in mid-afternoon. After sunset, temperatures steadily decline on clear nights with the tremendous loss of heat through reradiation. The minimum for the day generally is attained just after sunrise, although this pattern is disrupted when skies become overcast or during the passage of a storm. The range of temperatures is much larger on clear, sunny days, when solar radiation quickly heats the ground but nighttime reradiation is similarly unobstructed, than on cloudy days. Thus, Nebraska's continental position and predominantly clear skies result in large daily temperature ranges.

Mountain Barriers

The contrast between the moderate temperatures of a maritime location and Nebraska's extreme fluctuations is accentuated by the mountains of western North America. The coastal chain and the Rocky Mountains greatly restrict the penetration of marine influence. Air crossing these barriers loses a considerable amount of water vapor as it rises, cools, and precipitates much of the moisture derived from the evaporation of Pacific waters.

To the east of the mountains the central continent is open to invasions of contrasting air masses from north and south. Cold arctic air frequently extends southward until it comes in contact with relatively warm, moist air from the Gulf of Mexico. The southerly and northerly penetration of these air mass types varies particularly with the seasons. In winter, polar air normally dominates Nebraska's weather, but with the lack of any land barrier to the south, unseasonably warm air frequently flows into the state from the south for short durations. Similarly, tropical summer air is often displaced by cooler, dry conditions emanating out of Canada. In both situations, the ameliorating temperatures provide welcome relief from the extremes of the season. No other continental area experiences the severe range of contrasting air mass conditions as the region between the Rocky Mountains and the Mississippi.

Nebraska's moisture pattern is similarly associated with the predominance of air mass types, for they are the principal source of water vapor, influence the mechanisms for inducing the condensation of clouds, and partially determine the spatial and temporal distribution of precipitation for the state.

Of the total moisture carried in the atmosphere over the United States, nearly half is condensed and precipitated as rain, snow, sleet, or hail by low-pressure systems (cyclonic disturbances), thunderstorms, or hurricanes. Because the source of this water vapor is primarily the Pacific or Gulf waters, annual precipitation is greatest along the mountain slopes of the Pacific coast and the Gulf coastal plain. The mountain ranges force moisture-bearing air from the west to rise, cool, and precipitate most of its moisture before it enters the state as modified Pacific air. Consequently, Nebraska derives most of its precipitable moisture from summer incursions of tropical Gulf air. The sea-sonal precipitation distribution demonstrates this effect (fig. 2). Over 80 percent of the summer rainfall of a triangular area from South Dakota, Nebraska, and Kansas to Illinois is associated with frontal systems of dissimilar air masses. This aspect of precipitation will be discussed more extensively in the section on atmospheric humidity and precipitation.

Pressure Systems and Atmospheric Motion

Atmospheric circulation is analogous to a giant heat machine which is maintained by the temperature difference existing between the equatorial zone and the polar regions. The unequal distribution of solar energy over the spherical earth creates vertical and horizontal variations in pressure. Comparatively small horizontal pressure differences produce strong surface winds, while greater vertical differences result in weaker air currents due to the effect of gravity on a column of air.

Warm air has a lower density than cold air; thus, if the earth had a homogeneous surface and did not rotate, warm air near the equator would constantly be replaced by cold air from the polar regions. Surface winds would blow toward the equator from the poles, converge, and, having become warm, would rise and return toward the poles in the upper air flow. Under those circumstances Nebraska would experience consistent chilling northerly winds. Because the earth rotates and does not have a homogeneous surface, however, the flow of air is also influenced by other forces such as deflective and centripetal forces due to the earth's rotation and temperature differences between land and water.

In general, surface air in tropical regions tends to move toward the equator in a westerly direction, rise at the equator, and move poleward aloft to about 30° north and south latitude, where it sinks. The subsiding air at those latitudes is associated with higher surface pressure and clear skies.

As a result of the sinking motion, subtropical region, lower-level air now diverges, much of it returning toward the equator and part of it moving poleward toward a subpolar low-pressure zone created by the earth's motion. Rotational deflection causes surface winds to blow generally from west to east in the hemispheric zones of roughly between 30° and 60° latitude (Nebraska is located between 40° and 43° north latitude). Thus, in Nebraska, most of the surface winds have an eastward component, commonly blowing from the southwest, west, or northwest rather than the east. These winds are not as consistent as those of the tropics, however, because storm systems or eddies often form in this zone of confrontation of dissimilar air masses.

Nebraska's climate is not simply a synopsis of weather data and statistics, nor is it static. One should consider it as the summary of all statistical weather information, with spatial and temporal variations determined by these generalized climatic controls.

MERLIN P. LAWSON

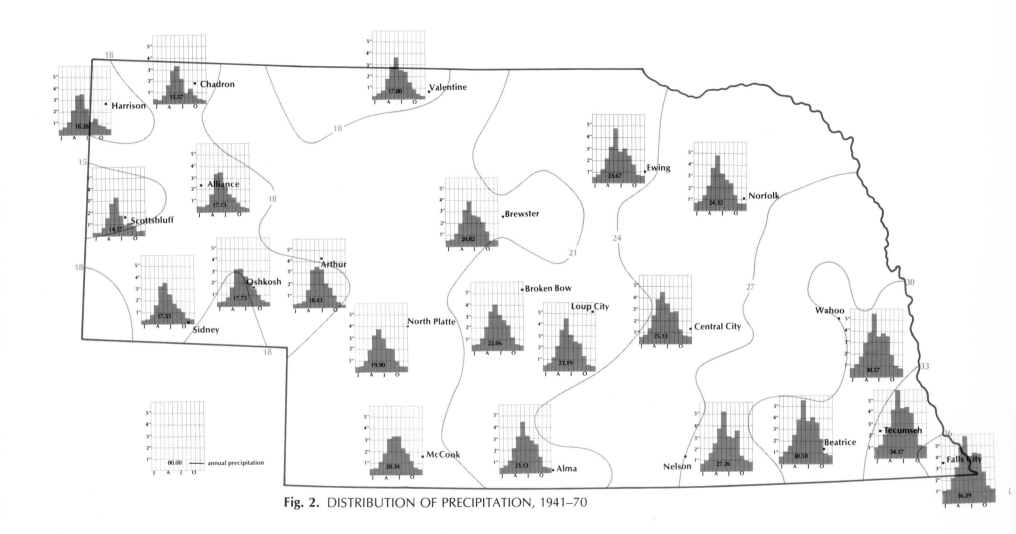

Fig. 2. DISTRIBUTION OF PRECIPITATION, 1941–70

NEBRASKA'S WEATHER STATIONS

The act of Congress establishing the Weather Bureau (now called the National Weather Service) as of July 1, 1891, provided for "the taking of such meteorological observations as may be necessary to establish and record climatic conditions in the United States." Before that time, there were only a few locations where climatological data were collected on a continuous basis, and those locations were found primarily in the more populated eastern states. Early attempts to characterize Nebraska's climate were made by army Medical and Signal Service personnel who recorded weather data at military posts in Nebraska Territory. Although these data were collected on an irregular basis and lacked a high degree of standardization, they have been extremely valuable in attempts to assess the climate of Nebraska during the nineteenth century.

In general, two types of weather station networks have been established since the creation of the Weather Service: a first-order station network and a substation network. There are currently 266 first-order stations (also termed National Weather Service Offices) in the United States, all manned by full-time, paid National Weather Service personnel. Their basic responsibilities are the collection of hourly surface meteorological data, preparation of aviation briefings, the issuance of severe weather warnings for surrounding counties, and public service (that is, the issuance of specific

Weather observation station at Arthur, Nebraska, typical of many of the approximately 300 operated by volunteers in the state. (Photo by Merlin P. Lawson)

forecast information to the media or interested individuals).

Nebraska has seven first-order stations, located at the airports in Omaha, Lincoln, Grand Island, Norfolk, North Platte, Valentine, and Scottsbluff. In addition to the basic responsibilities outlined above, several of these stations have supplemental duties. The Omaha, Grand Island, Norfolk, North Platte, and Scottsbluff stations also operate weather radar, collecting data on the movement of precipitation cells across the state. Of the five radar installations, Grand Island has the most powerful radar, with an effective range covering most of the state. Upper air observations are regularly taken at North Platte and Omaha.

Finally, in the hierarchy of first-order stations in Nebraska, Omaha has been designated as state forecast office. It is the responsibility of the National Weather Service Office in Omaha to issue aviation and general public weather forecasts for the entire

state. These forecasts are then modified by each of the other first-order stations to reflect regional variations in expected weather conditions. Fire-weather forecasts and stream-flood forecasts for the state are prepared in the Omaha weather office, which is also one of the few locations in Nebraska where solar radiation data and evaporation data are collected on a regular basis.

Field instrumentation pictured at the Grand Island first-order weather station includes a thermal shelter, rain gauges, and evaporation pan, with radar tower in the background. (Photo by Merlin P. Lawson)

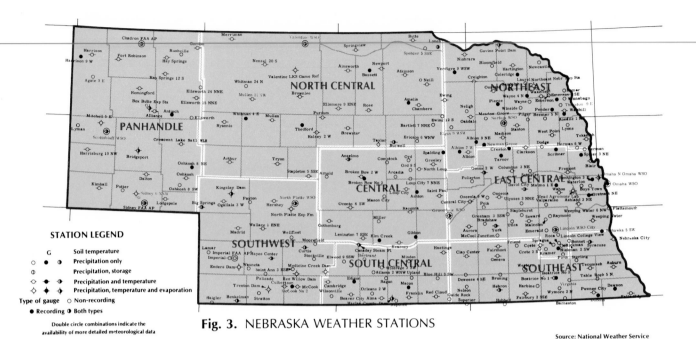

STATION LEGEND

G Soil temperature

○ ● ◐ Precipitation only

◎ Precipitation, storage

◇ ◆ ◑ Precipitation and temperature

◇ ◆ ◑ Precipitation, temperature and evaporation

Type of gauge ○ Non-recording

● Recording ◐ Both types

Double circle combinations indicate the
availability of more detailed meteorological data

Fig. 3. NEBRASKA WEATHER STATIONS

Source: National Weather Service

Substations, which constitute the second type of weather station network, provide abridged reports and perform related functions which supplement the more complete data collecting done by the first-order stations. A significant feature of substations is that they are operated by unpaid volunteers. Their primary duty is to provide a daily record of the precipitation, temperature, or other meteorological phenomena observed. These data serve, for example, as the basis for climatic, hydrologic, agricultural, aviation, air pollution, and engineering research. Under the substation system, the National Weather Service provides the instruments for observations taken by over 12,000 volunteer observers and is further assisted by approximately 1,400 other persons and agencies which make available to the National Weather Service climatological data from their own instruments. Figure 3 shows the names and locations of the substations in Nebraska.

The design specifications for instruments used in collecting weather data, as well as the procedure to be followed in their utilization, have been standardized by international agreement of the World Meteorological Organization. Standardization is essential to ensure that climatic data can be compared from region to region and from country to country.

A description of weather instruments must begin with the *instrument shelter*, a boxlike structure designed to protect certain meteorological instruments from exposure to direct sunshine, precipitation, and condensation, while at the same time providing adequate ventilation. Instrument shelters are painted white, have louvered sides, usually a double roof with an air space between, and are mounted on a stand approximately 4 feet (1.2 meters) above the ground. The door of the shelter faces north and the shelter should be located away from any physical structure.

Temperature Measurements. Temperature is a relative term which indicates the capacity to transfer heat by conduction. For comparative purposes, a scale of temperatures

8

must be defined; the two fixed points usually selected to define such a scale are the boiling point and freezing point of pure water under standard atmospheric pressure. The Fahrenheit (F.) scale has traditionally been employed by climatologists in the United States, but under the direction of the National Weather Service, the Celsius, or Centigrade, (C.) scale is now slowly being adopted. The freezing point is 32° F. or 0° C. and the boiling point 212° F. or 100° C. Conversions from Fahrenheit to Centigrade and vice versa can be made using these formulas:

°F. = 9/5 °C. + 32°
°C. = 5/9 (°F. − 32°)

Four instruments for measuring temperature are commonly found in an instrument shelter: the *mercurial thermometer*, used to measure the air temperature at any given moment; a *maximum thermometer*, designed so that it registers the maximum temperature attained during a specified period of time; a *minimum thermometer*, designed to register automatically the lowest temperature attained during a specified period of time; and an automatically recording thermometer, called a *thermograph*, which draws a continuous temperature record on a piece of graph paper.

Humidity Measurements. Humidity refers to the amount of water vapor, or water in gas form, in the atmosphere. The amount of most gases in the atmosphere is relatively constant throughout the world. However, the percentage of water vapor varies from nearly zero to more than 4 percent of the

Cooling of the Atmosphere

total atmospheric pressure and is extremely important to the climate of a region.

Relative humidity, normally stated as a percentage, represents the amount of water vapor actually in the air compared with the maximum that the air can hold at a given temperature and pressure. The atmospheric capacity for moisture varies directly with temperature; the higher the temperature, the greater the ability to contain water vapor. When the relative humidity reaches 100

percent, the air is said to be saturated. Air that is not saturated becomes so if it is sufficiently cooled, even though no additional water vapor is added. For this reason, dew drops frequently condense on vegetation or automobiles on calm summer evenings as the warm air comes in contact with cooler surfaces. When temperatures fall below 32° F. (0° C.), condensed water vapor forms frost.

The most useful instrument for determining relative humidity is the *sling psychrometer*, which consists of two ventilated thermometers mounted side by side. One of the thermometers has a moistened wick around its bulb. As long as the air is unsaturated, water evaporates from the wick, causing the temperature to drop below that recorded on the ordinary thermometer. Ventilation is obtained by swinging the mounted thermometers, which are attached to a swivel joint. The rate of evaporation depends upon the dryness of the air; thus the temperature difference between the two thermometers increases as the relative humidity decreases. The difference between the wet- and dry-bulb temperatures is read, and from standard psychrometric tables the relative humidity and the dew point temperature can be obtained. A *hygrograph* located within the instrument shelter records humidity data.

Pressure Measurements. The instrument commonly used to measure atmospheric pressure is a barometer. The *mercurial barometer*, the standard type, is based on a refinement of a simple principle involving a glass tube, sealed at the upper end and having its open end inverted in a dish of mercury. Atmospheric pressure balances the weight of the mercury column. A more convenient instrument is the *aneroid barometer*, which is found in many homes. It consists of a hollow metal chamber partly emptied of air and sealed. The chamber walls are flexible so that the chamber expands or contracts as outside pressure varies. These movements operate an indicator read against a calibrated dial. The *barograph* incorporates a pen and arm allowing a continuous record of air pressure to be kept on a clock-driven drum. Rising or high pressure values are associated with clearing or fair weather, while a falling or low pressure indicates stormy weather.

Wind Measurements. Wind direction and speed are observed primarily by first-order weather stations. Wind direction is determined by a *wind vane* or *aerovane* and wind speed is measured by an *anemometer*. Both instruments are located on a tower exactly 10 meters (approximately 33 feet) above the ground for purposes of standardization. Many aerovane and anemometer systems are connected to graph recorders to collect continuous wind data.

Precipitation Measurements. A number of standard gauges are employed to record rainfall. The *storage gauge* stores, but does not record, precipitation received in a twenty-four hour period, or for as long as an entire season in remote areas. Three recording gauges—the weighing rain gauge, the tipping bucket rain gauge, and the float type of rain gauge—are widely used to supply a complete record of the amount and timing of precipitation.

A weighing rain gauge consists of a receiver in the shape of a funnel which empties into a bucket mounted on a weighing mechanism. The weight of the catch is recorded, on a clock-driven chart, as inches of precipitation. This type of gauge is frequently used at the substations in Nebraska's data network. The *tipping bucket* gauge allows rain water to flow from the receiving funnel into a triangular bucket which is half of a two-bucket receptacle pivoted on a knife-edge. When the right-hand bucket fills to a specified amount, it drops down, closes a switch, and brings the left-hand side of the receptacle under the funnel while the water on the right-hand side drains out. When the left-hand side fills, the procedure is repeated. The buckets are usually calibrated to tip after 0.01 inch or 1.0 millimeter has accumulated, and each electrical contact is recorded and represents that amount of rainfall. Float gauges are essentially water-level gauges. A float in the gauge receptacle rises as rain water enters the chamber, the rise of the float being recorded by a pen on a calibrated clock-driven chart. Recently, computer digital tape has been used on recording gauges instead of charts, easing the laborious task of chart reading.

Snowfall is measured by taking a "representative" sample of snow depths around the observation station with a yardstick. The interpretation of a representative sample varies widely, leading to a lack of standardization in the collection of snowfall data. Moreover, under windy snowfall conditions, the wind may completely remove the snow from an observation station as quickly as it accumulates on the ground and pile it up in large drifts along the side of buildings, ditches, or snow fences. During blizzard conditions, therefore, observers must estimate the amount of snow which has fallen, without any direct measurement. Because of these problems, records of snowfall must be used with caution.

Evaporation Measurements. Evaporation, the least measured indicator of weather, is usually measured by pans of water from which daily or weekly loss is measured. Evaporation pans may be floated on a raft on a body of water, sunk in the ground so their water level is even with the surface of the ground, or installed on low stands above the ground (the most common method). The *class A evaporation pan* is approximately 4 feet (1.2 meters) in diameter, 10 inches (25 centimeters) deep, and is mounted near the ground on supports which permit a free flow of air around and under the pan. On rainy days, rainfall measured by a standard gauge must be considered in arriving at the evaporation estimate. Once the amount of evaporation has been determined by reading the level of the water on a thin calibrated rod in the pan, the water level is returned to the zero mark and left until the next observation time.

KENNETH F. DEWEY

2
Temperature

Cold Winters
A Winter Discomfort Index
Heating Degree-Days
Hot Summers
Cooling Degree-Days
Livestock Stress
Sunshine
The Progression of Spring across Nebraska
The Freeze-Free Season
The Agroclimatic Calendar

COLD WINTERS

Although winter officially begins in the Northern Hemisphere on December 21, the shortest day of the year and the time when the sun's rays are farthest south of the Equator, and ends the second that the direct rays of the sun pass north of the Equator on March 21, such precise astronomic calculations are obviously a gross oversimplification of these seasons in terms of the temperatures that may be expected.

The chill of winter temperatures first enters Nebraska from the northwest (fig. 4). Indoor heat usually is first needed in that part of the state during the first week in September and may be required for comfort until mid-June. The 280-day "heating season" in western Nebraska is four times longer than the 90-day (December 21–March 21) astronomical winter.

On the basis of below-freezing temperatures, winter may range from 169 days in western Nebraska to less than 147 days in the east (fig. 5). If winter is defined as the number of days when the highest temperature is below freezing, the northeastern part of the state, with 53 days, has the longest season (fig. 6).

Few people will question that temperatures of 0° F. or below indicate winter. Different regions of the state average from fewer than ten to over twenty-two such days per year (fig. 7). Northeastern Nebraska, the coldest part of the state, has experienced runs of thirty consecutive days with temperatures below 0° and −5° F. (−18° and −21° C.) (figs. 9–10). Periods of one week or more with temperatures of −10° F. (−23° C.) or colder are not uncommon in the northern half of the state (fig. 11).

Extreme variation is characteristic of Nebraska's weather, however, and brief warm spells can be expected in winter. For example, at Culbertson, in the southwestern part of the state, temperatures in the high 60s and low 70s F. (low 20s C.) in January and high 70s and low 80s F. (high 20s C.) in February are not uncommon. Broken Bow in the Sandhills demonstrates the temperature range that can occur in midwinter: a high of 78° F. (26° C.) was recorded on January 30, 1896, while on January 28, 1915, the temperature fell to −42° F. (−41° C.).

RALPH E. NEILD

OCTOBER

NOVEMBER

Fig. 4. MEAN MONTHLY TEMPERATURES, OCTOBER–MARCH, 1941–70

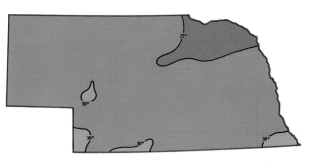

DECEMBER

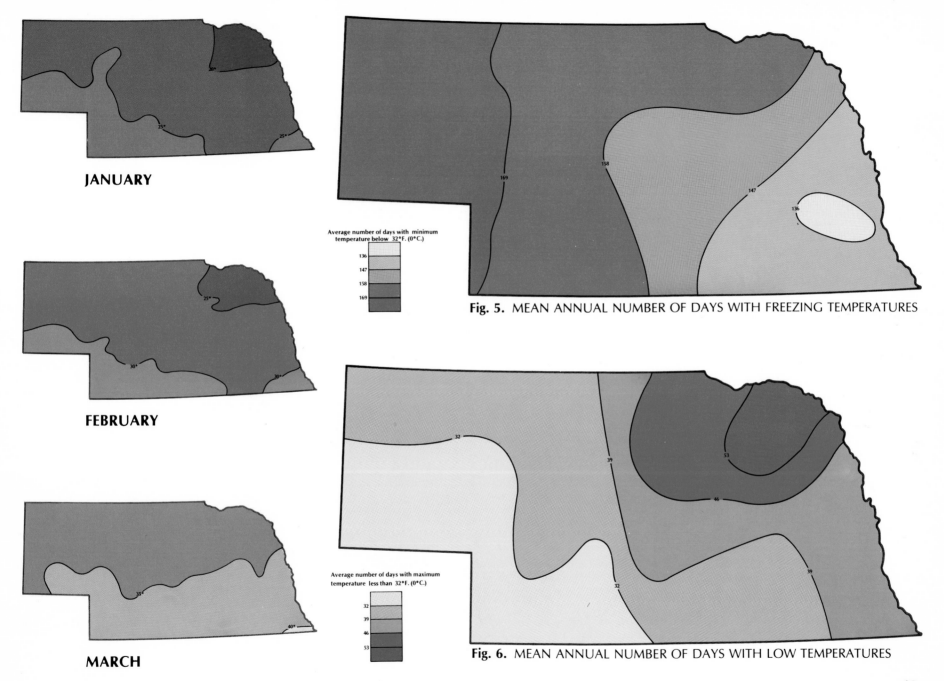

JANUARY

FEBRUARY

MARCH

Average number of days with minimum
temperature below 32°F. (0°C.)

136
147
158
169

Fig. 5. MEAN ANNUAL NUMBER OF DAYS WITH FREEZING TEMPERATURES

Average number of days with maximum
temperature less than 32°F. (0°C.)

32
39
46
53

Fig. 6. MEAN ANNUAL NUMBER OF DAYS WITH LOW TEMPERATURES

13

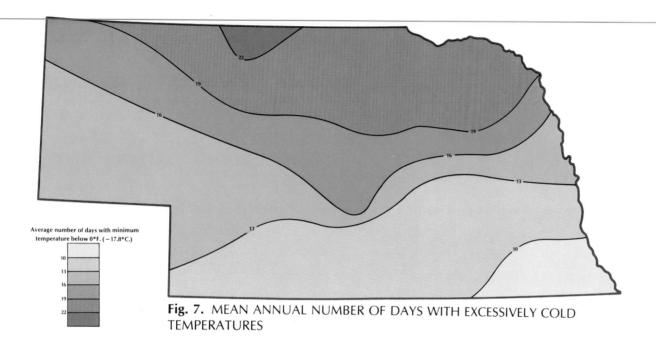

Fig. 7. MEAN ANNUAL NUMBER OF DAYS WITH EXCESSIVELY COLD TEMPERATURES

Average number of days with minimum
temperature below 0°F. (−17.8°C.)

10
13
16
19
22

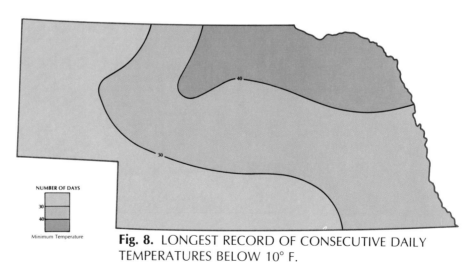

NUMBER OF DAYS

30
40

Minimum Temperature

Fig. 8. LONGEST RECORD OF CONSECUTIVE DAILY TEMPERATURES BELOW 10° F.

14

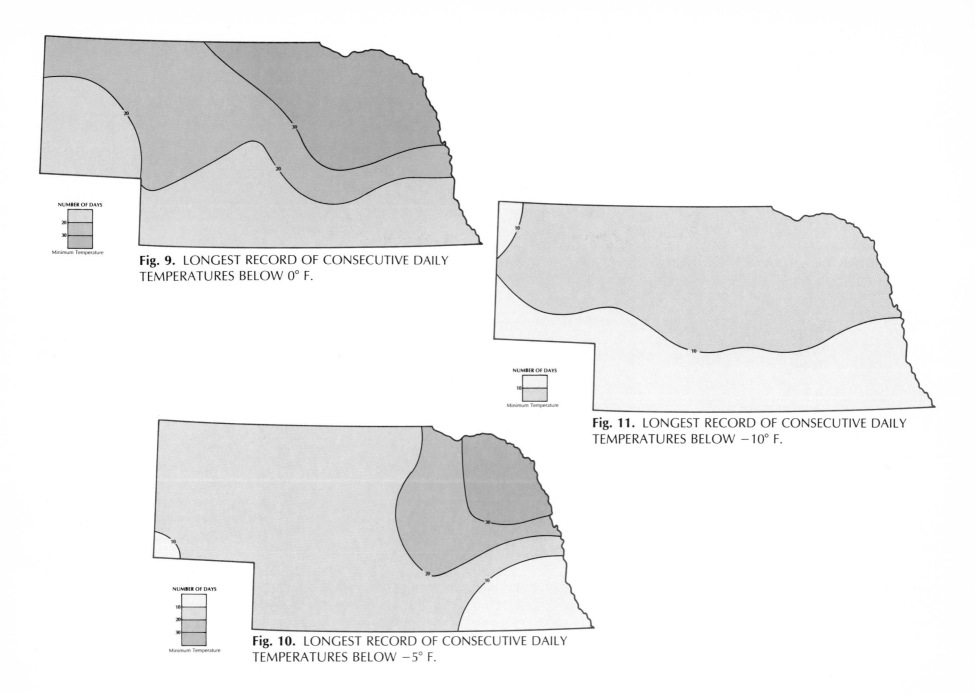

NUMBER OF DAYS

20
30

Minimum Temperature

Fig. 9. LONGEST RECORD OF CONSECUTIVE DAILY TEMPERATURES BELOW 0° F.

NUMBER OF DAYS

10

Minimum Temperature

Fig. 11. LONGEST RECORD OF CONSECUTIVE DAILY TEMPERATURES BELOW −10° F.

NUMBER OF DAYS

10
20
30

Minimum Temperature

Fig. 10. LONGEST RECORD OF CONSECUTIVE DAILY TEMPERATURES BELOW −5° F.

15

Table 2. Wind Chill Index

A WINTER DISCOMFORT INDEX

During the winter months Nebraskans are often exposed to chilling temperatures combined with blustery winds. With higher wind speeds, warm, moist air close to the surface of the skin is continually removed, promoting greater evaporation and reducing skin temperatures. The increased heat loss causes a person to feel cooler than he would in still air at the same temperature. A measure of the effect of various wind and temperature combinations on the exposed flesh is known as the wind chill index.

A number of comfort indices have been devised to measure wind chill equivalent temperatures, but the one most commonly used by the National Weather Service was devised by the late Paul Siple, the well-known geographer and Antarctic explorer. The sense of cold in the hands or face increases as the wind speed becomes greater. Table 2 shows that on a day with an air temperature of 20° F. (−7° C.) and a thirty-mile-per-hour wind, exposed skin surfaces would feel as though it were −18° F. (−28° C.). Persons working or playing outdoors should keep in mind that experiments show exposed flesh freezes under the following temperature-wind relationships:

20° F. (−7° C.) and 45 miles/hour
10° F. (−12° C.) and 18 miles/hour
−10° F. (−24° C.) and 7 miles/hour
−40° F. (−40° C.) and 2 miles/hour

AIR TEMPERATURE (° F.)																
35	30	25	20	15	10	5	0	−5	−10	−15	−20	−25	−30	−35	−40	−45
Wind Chill Equivalent Temperature																
4: 35	30	25	20	15	10	5	0	−5	−10	−15	−20	−25	−30	−35	−40	−45
5: 32	27	22	16	11	6	0	−5	−10	−15	−21	−26	−31	−36	−42	−47	−52
10: 22	16	10	3	−3	−9	−15	−22	−27	−34	−40	−46	−52	−58	−64	−71	−77
15: 16	9	2	−5	−11	−18	−25	−31	−38	−45	−51	−58	−65	−72	−78	−85	−92
20: 12	4	−3	−10	−17	−24	−31	−39	−46	−53	−60	−67	−74	−81	−88	−95	−103
25: 8	1	−7	−15	−22	−29	−36	−44	−51	−59	−66	−74	−81	−88	−96	−103	−110
30: 6	−2	−10	−18	−25	−33	−41	−49	−56	−64	−71	−79	−86	−93	−101	−109	−116
35: 4	−4	−12	−20	−27	−35	−43	−52	−58	−67	−74	−82	−89	−97	−105	−113	−120
40: 3	−5	−13	−21	−29	−37	−45	−53	−60	−69	−76	−84	−92	−100	−107	−115	−123
45: 2	−6	−14	−22	−30	−38	−46	−54	−62	−70	−78	−85	−93	−102	−109	−117	−125

Wind Speed (Miles per Hour). Zones: COLD, VERY COLD, BITTER COLD, EXTREME COLD.

Wind speeds greater than 40 MPH have little additional chilling effect.

SOURCE: National Weather Service.

Many homes are equipped with an outdoor thermometer, but few have instruments for accurately measuring wind. If you have a thermometer and would like to calculate the wind chill factor, the following indicators can be used for estimating wind speed:

1–3 miles/hour: smoke drifts to indicate direction

4–7 miles/hour: leaves rustle and you can feel the wind on your face

8–12 miles/hour: flags are extended and leaves and small twigs move on trees and shrubs

13–18 miles/hour: dust and loose papers are blown; small branches move

19–24 miles/hour: small leafless branches are in constant motion

25–31 miles/hour: large branches move and overhead wires whistle

32–38 miles/hour: trees move; walking is difficult

39–46 miles/hour: walking is impeded and small branches and twigs break

over 46 miles/hour: structural and tree damage is possible; no matter what the temperature, you probably should remain indoors

Unfortunately, weather conditions do not always cooperate with the work schedules of Nebraska farmers, ranchers, and many other people engaged in outdoor occupations. Thus, the effect of extended periods of cold on the body should be recognized as a safety precaution.

Hypothermia. A cold stroke can result when the body is subjected to excessive chilling. If the body temperature drops to 95° F. (35° C.), people tend to become sluggish and inactive. Unless immediate rapid and then slower rewarming of the body occurs, death may result from heart failure.

Frostbite. Freezing of body tissues results when the blood supply to exposed areas does not replenish heat loss. As the damaged tissues become white or blue in color, circulation is further hampered. Thawing allows body fluids to move into the tissues, which become swollen and extremely painful.

Trench foot. This disorder commonly occurs when cold and wet conditions are combined. Temperatures do not have to be below freezing for extremities such as the feet to become swollen to the point of developing gangrene. Insulated boots, designed to absorb perspiration as well as protect against the cold, should prevent trench foot.

MERLIN P. LAWSON

(Photo by Debbie Ivey)

17

HEATING DEGREE-DAYS

The concept of heating degree-days—the number of degrees per day that the average temperature is below 65° F. (18° C.)—is commonly used by people who deal with heating and fuel requirements: by heating engineers in designing more effective heating systems, utility companies in estimating heating fuel needs, and government agencies in establishing a basis for fuel allocation. The amount of heating energy required is directly proportional to the heating degree-days; thus, to maintain the same temperature in the same building, twice as much fuel is used on a day when the temperature averages 45° F. (7° C.) as on a day averaging 55° F. (13° C.). Ordinarily the daily temperature first averages below 65° F. during the first week in September in the northwest, the second week of September in the central, and about the third week of September in the southeastern part of Nebraska (fig. 12). The average annual number of heating degree-days increases from 5,800 in the southeast to over 7,400 in the northwest (fig. 13). This map shows that similar homes in Omaha, Lincoln, Hastings, and Red Cloud have similar heating requirements, since these locations average between 5,800 and 6,200 heating degree-days. By comparison, Fairbanks, Alaska, averages 14,158 heating degree-days and Phoenix, Arizona, only 1,492. A home in Gordon in the northwest would require about 28 percent more fuel than a similar home at Falls

18

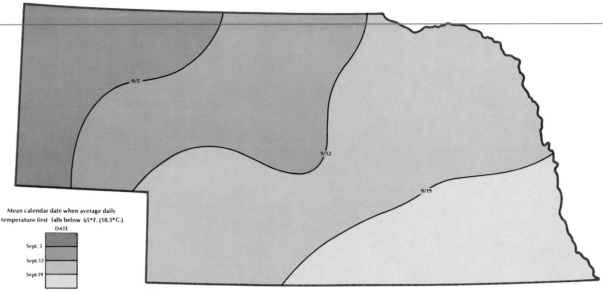

Mean calendar date when average daily temperature first falls below 65°F. (18.3°C.)

DATE

Sept. 5
Sept. 12
Sept. 19

Fig. 12. MEAN DATE OF FIRST INDOOR HEATING

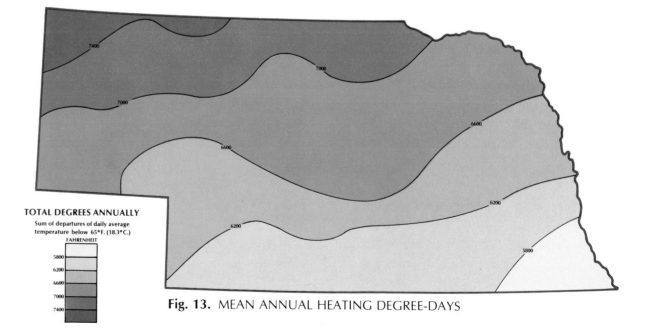

TOTAL DEGREES ANNUALLY

Sum of departures of daily average temperature below 65°F. (18.3°C.)

FAHRENHEIT

5800
6200
6600
7000
7400

Fig. 13. MEAN ANNUAL HEATING DEGREE-DAYS

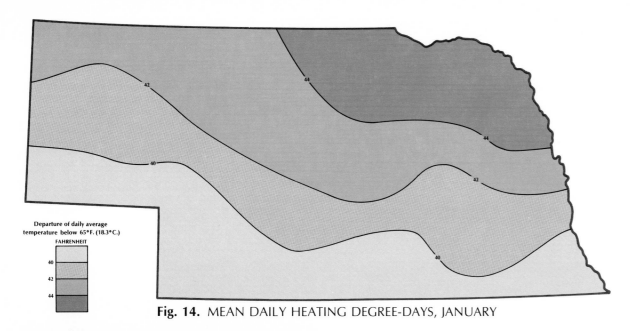

Departure of daily average
temperature below 65°F. (18.3°C.)

FAHRENHEIT

40
42
44

Fig. 14. MEAN DAILY HEATING DEGREE-DAYS, JANUARY

City in the southeast because of the difference in number of heating degree-days (7,400 vs. 5,800).

Northwestern Nebraska has the highest winter heating requirement, but the northeast needs the most heat in January (fig. 14). During January, the coldest month, the southern tier of counties averages less than forty heating degrees per day. Areas north of that tier of counties are progressively colder and have a greater need for heating fuel. On an average January day, 10 percent more fuel is required to heat buildings in northeastern Nebraska than those of similar construction in the southern part of the state.

RALPH E. NEILD

(Photo by Gary Shapiro)

HOT SUMMERS

Like winter, summer is a season of temperature extremes in Nebraska's continental climate (fig. 15). The record of Hartington in the northeast contains examples of such seasonal extremes: the record low of −38° F. (−39° C.) on January 12, 1912, and high of 118° F. (50° C.) on July 17, 1936, result in a range of 156° F. (77° C.). Nineteen thirty-six was the year for record highs; there were over seventeen days with temperatures above 100° F (38° C.) at Hartington. It was also a year for record lows in February; the temperatures on the fifteenth and twentieth were −25° F. (−32° C.) and −22° F. (−30° C.), respectively.

By the astronomical calendar, summer begins on June 22, but average temperatures become warm enough to require artificial cooling for comfort in southeastern Nebraska during the last week in May (fig. 22). Brief unseasonably hot spells are not uncommon in late March and April. Fairbury, in the south, has recorded six days with temperatures of 90° F. (32° C.) or higher in March and over 100° F. (38° C.) in April. Temperatures of 100° F. or higher have been recorded on all except two days in June at Fairbury.

South-central Nebraska averages over fifty days per year with temperatures above 90° F., compared to less than twenty such days in the north and northwestern parts of the

Fig. 15. MEAN MONTHLY TEMPERATURES, APRIL–SEPTEMBER, 1941–70

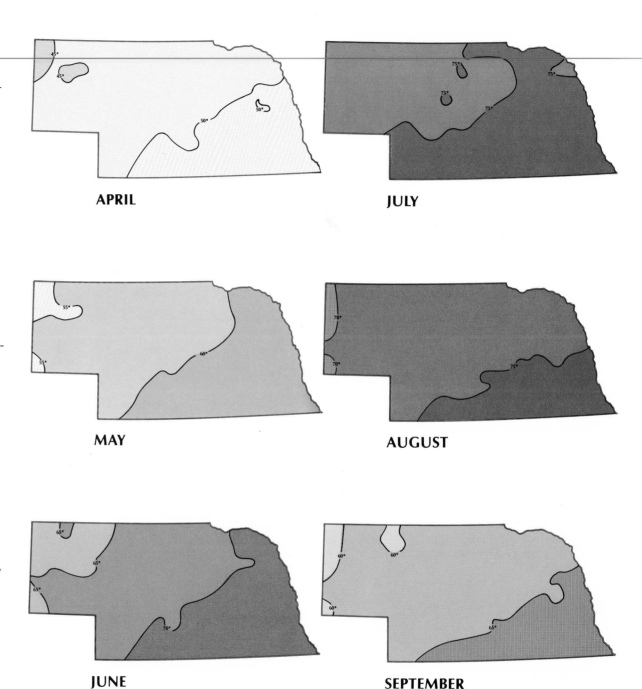

APRIL

JULY

MAY

AUGUST

JUNE

SEPTEMBER

state (fig. 16). Extended hot spells with temperatures in the mid-90s for a month or more, above 100° F. for three weeks, or 104° F. (40° C.) or higher for a week are not uncommon (figs. 17–20).

The summers of 1901, 1913, and 1934 were particularly hot. In 1901 there were twenty-two consecutive days (July 7–July 28) when the temperature at Fairbury was 100° F. or higher. In 1913, the temperature was 90° F. or higher from August 1 to September 9. In 1934, afternoon temperatures reached 104° F. or higher every day for a two-week period from July 9 to July 22. During that time it was 111° F. (44° C.), 113° F. (45° C.), and 110° F. (43° C.), respectively, on July 13, 15, and 19.

RALPH E. NEILD

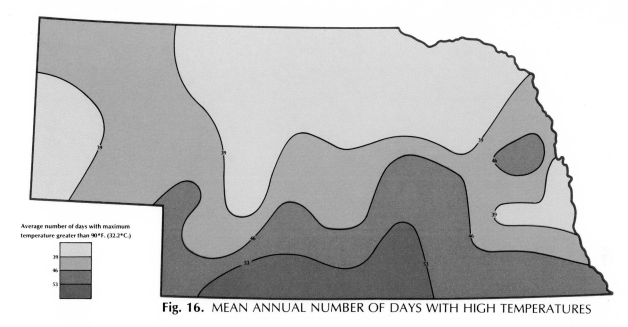

Average number of days with maximum temperature greater than 90° F. (32.2° C.)

39
46
53

Fig. 16. MEAN ANNUAL NUMBER OF DAYS WITH HIGH TEMPERATURES

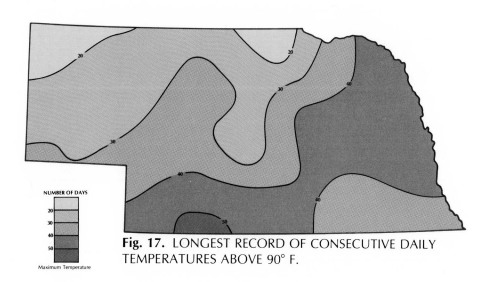

NUMBER OF DAYS

20
30
40
50

Maximum Temperature

Fig. 17. LONGEST RECORD OF CONSECUTIVE DAILY TEMPERATURES ABOVE 90° F.

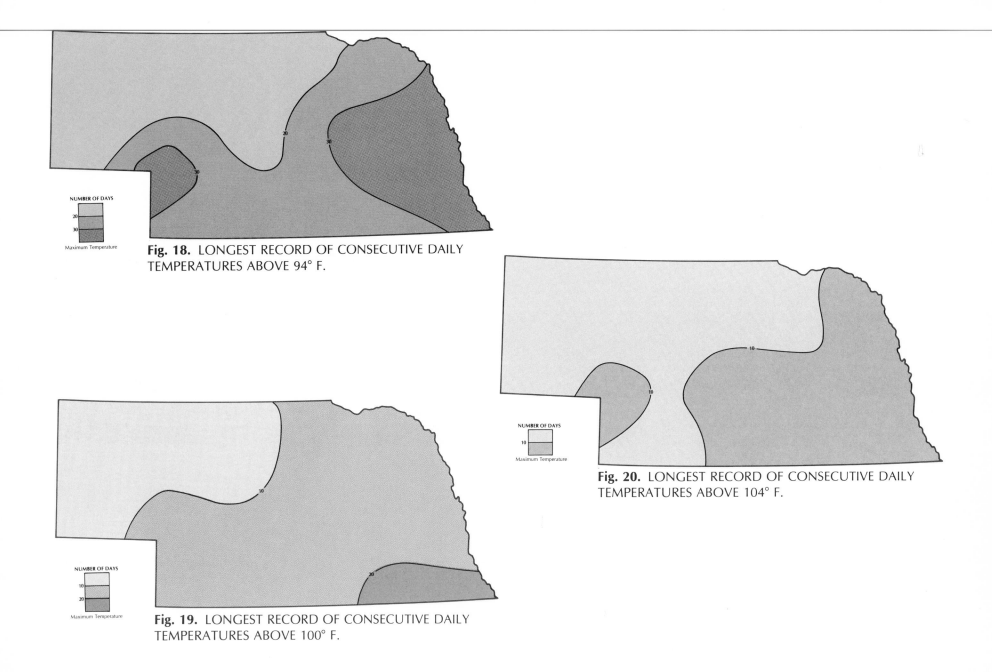

Fig. 18. LONGEST RECORD OF CONSECUTIVE DAILY TEMPERATURES ABOVE 94° F.

NUMBER OF DAYS
20
30
Maximum Temperature

Fig. 19. LONGEST RECORD OF CONSECUTIVE DAILY TEMPERATURES ABOVE 100° F.

NUMBER OF DAYS
10
20
Maximum Temperature

Fig. 20. LONGEST RECORD OF CONSECUTIVE DAILY TEMPERATURES ABOVE 104° F.

NUMBER OF DAYS
10
Maximum Temperature

22

COOLING DEGREE-DAYS

Cooling degree-days indicate cooling requirements just as heating degree-days are used to measure the need for heat. The base temperature for cooling degree-days is 65° F. (18° C.), as it is for heating degree-days, and the manner of calculation is the same except that cooling degree-days are figured with temperatures above 65° F. For example, on a day with an average temperature 20° F. (11° C.) above 65° F. (18° C.), twice as much energy would be required to artificially cool a home or office as on a day with an average temperature only 10° F. (5.5° C.) above 65° F. (18° C.).

Figures 21 and 23 show southeastern Nebraska to have two and one-half times the cooling requirement of the northeastern part of the state in July. Comparison of the heating and cooling degree-day maps shows the need for heating energy to be 5.8 times the need for cooling energy in the southeast (5,800 heating degree-days vs. 1,000 cooling degree-days). The requirement for heating energy is eighteen and one-half times that for cooling energy in the extreme northwest. Data such as these indicate not only the relative need for different types of air conditioning but also the energy requirements for their operation.

RALPH E. NEILD

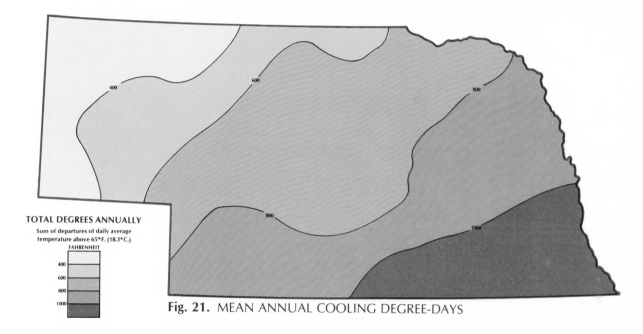

TOTAL DEGREES ANNUALLY

Sum of departures of daily average
temperature above 65°F. (18.3°C.)

FAHRENHEIT

	400
	600
	800
	1000

Fig. 21. MEAN ANNUAL COOLING DEGREE-DAYS

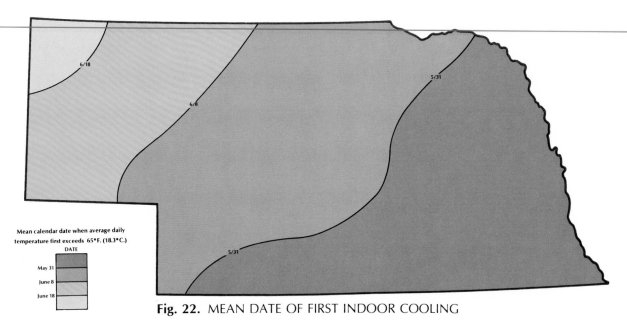

Mean calendar date when average daily
temperature first exceeds 65°F. (18.3°C.)

DATE

May 31
June 8
June 18

Fig. 22. MEAN DATE OF FIRST INDOOR COOLING

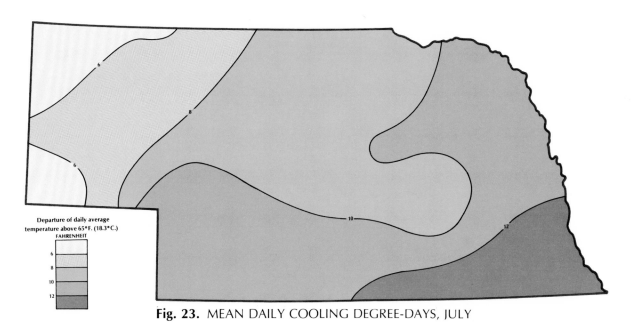

Departure of daily average
temperature above 65°F. (18.3°C.)

FAHRENHEIT

6
8
10
12

Fig. 23. MEAN DAILY COOLING DEGREE-DAYS, JULY

LIVESTOCK STRESS

Livestock stress occurs when animals are subjected to prolonged periods of temperatures above 80° F. (27° C.), particularly when the humidity is high. Such conditions result in lower feed efficiency in meat animals and reduced milk production in dairy cattle. For example, a two-hundred-pound pig that gains two pounds a day when the temperature is 70° F. (21° C.) will begin to lose weight at temperatures above 95° F. (35° C.) and may die if an attempt is made at shipping it to market. The heat-regulating mechanism in dairy cows begins to fail at temperatures of about 80° F. and milk production decreases in direct proportion to the number of hours per day when the temperature is above that level. Periods of potential heat stress are now forecast so that measures may be taken to prevent adverse effects. The provision of shade and cool water and exposure to cooling breezes are among the most effective means of reducing heat stress.

The average number of days in the summer when the temperature is 80° F. (27° C.) or higher (fig. 24) decreases from over 110 in the south to less than 70 in the northwestern part of the state. The number of hours per day with temperatures above 80° F. has a similar pattern (table 3), ranging from an average of fewer than four in the northwest to about ten in the south during late July, the hottest time of the year.

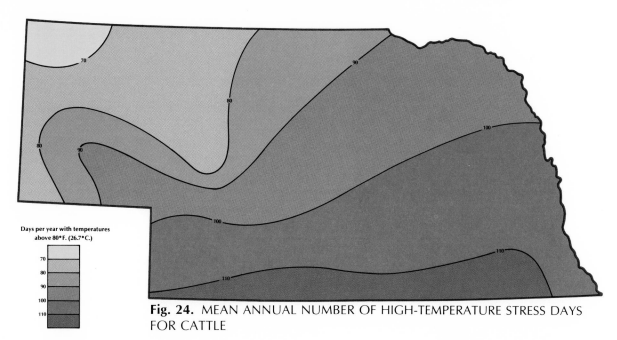

Fig. 24. MEAN ANNUAL NUMBER OF HIGH-TEMPERATURE STRESS DAYS FOR CATTLE

Days per year with temperatures above 80° F. (26.7° C.)

70
80
90
100
110

Late winter storms, particularly those that occur during the calving season in March, may also be hazardous to livestock. Strong winds with blowing, drifting snow cause cattle to scatter and complicate feeding operations; and wet snow or cold rain and wind may fatally chill unprotected newborn calves.

RALPH E. NEILD

Table 3. Average Dates and Duration of Temperatures above 80° F. at Selected Locations

Station	Dates	Annual Duration		Temperatures from July 21 to July 31		
		Days	Hours	Daily Max.	Daily Min.	Hours per day above 80° F.
Benkelman	May 30–Sept. 22	116	687	93.0	62.0	9.3
Fairbury	May 31–Sept. 20	113	735	92.0	66.0	10.2
Franklin	June 6–Sept. 20	112	687	91.8	65.0	9.7
David City	June 6–Sept. 12	99	505	89.0	65.0	8.0
Hartington	June 8–Sept. 11	95	428	88.0	63.0	6.7
Broken Bow	June 10–Sept. 11	94	403	88.0	60.6	6.7
Halsey	June 9–Sept. 10	94	411	89.0	60.9	6.8
Gordon	June 5–Sept. 10	88	312	88.6	56.0	5.6
Atkinson	June 14–Sept. 8	87	428	88.0	62.0	6.5
Kimball	June 17–Sept. 6	82	267	88.0	56.0	5.3
Alliance	June 18–Sept. 6	81	281	88.0	58.0	5.6
Harrison	June 24–Sept. 9	71	180	86.0	54.7	3.8

SUNSHINE

The number of hours that sunshine is possible in central Nebraska varies from fifteen hours and nine minutes on June 22, the longest day, to nine hours and twelve minutes on December 21, the shortest day. An instrument called a sunshine recorder measures the amount of time each day that the earth is sunlit (because clouds sometimes obscure the sun, the earth's surface does not receive sunlight during all the daytime hours).

Measurements in Nebraska show that on an annual basis, the state is sunlit during about two-thirds of the daylight hours. The percentage of sunshine is highest during July, August, and September, when 68–76 percent of the daylight hours are sunny, and lowest in January, February, and March (52–66 percent).

North-central Nebraska receives more sunshine than other areas of the state. The western portion receives more sunshine during the winter months than the eastern, whereas the east receives more sunshine in the summer than the west.

RALPH E. NEILD

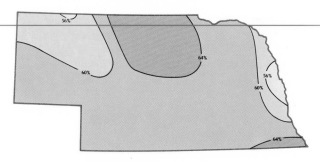

JANUARY

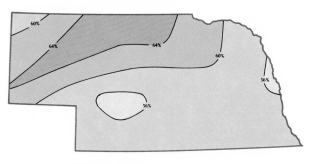

FEBRUARY

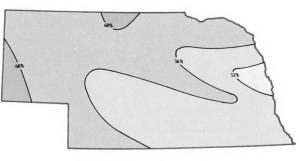

MARCH

Fig. 25. MEAN MONTHLY SUNSHINE (adapted from Norman J. Rosenberg, *Solar Energy and Sunshine in Nebraska*, Research Bulletin 213, Agricultural Experiment Station, University of Nebraska)

(Photo by Kathy Kuhlman)

26

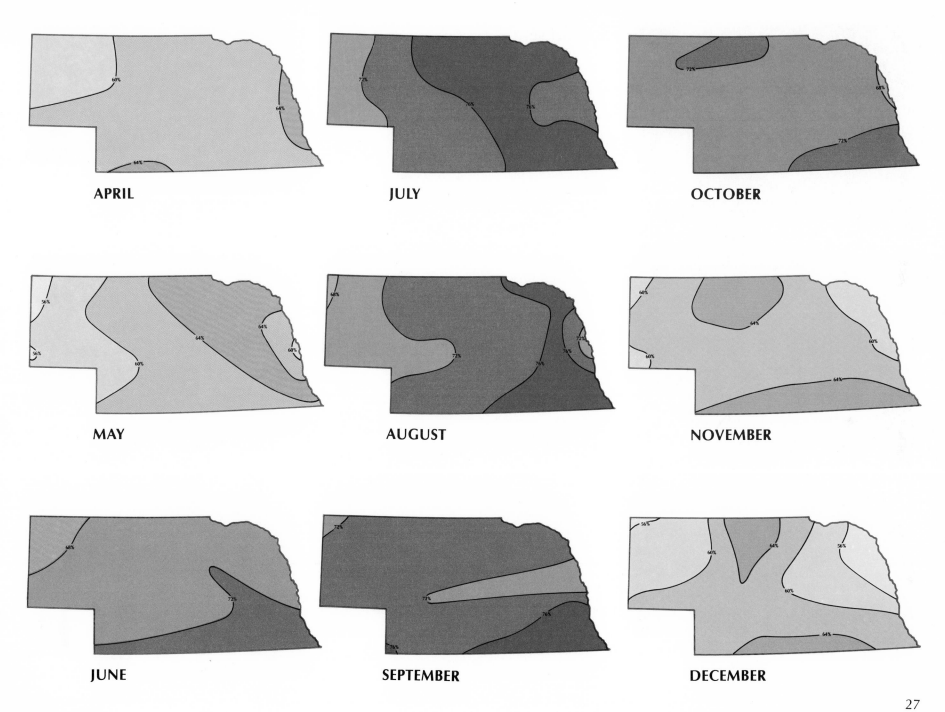

APRIL

JULY

OCTOBER

MAY

AUGUST

NOVEMBER

JUNE

SEPTEMBER

DECEMBER

27

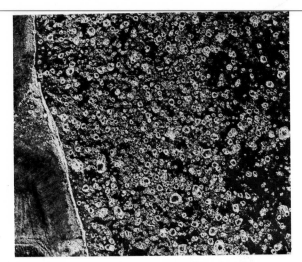

Aerial view of early spring ice floes on the Missouri River. (Photo by George Tuck)

THE PROGRESSION OF SPRING ACROSS NEBRASKA

Spring first enters the southeastern corner of Nebraska and progresses across the state in a northwesterly direction. It is a period of intense farming activity as 9,000,000 acres of crops and thousands of gardens are planted. Weather permitting, some oats, barley, and sugar beets may be planted in March, but most crops are planted in April and May. Different crops have different temperature requirements for germination and seedling growth, so there is a close relationship between time of planting and temperature for different regions. The temperature in extreme southern Nebraska averages about 45° F. (7° C.) during the first week in April. Potatoes, onions, lettuce, peas, carrots, and other cool-season vegetables may

safely be planted at this temperature. The southeastern third of Nebraska normally warms up to 50° F. (10° C.) by April 18, when the temperature in the northwest still averages below 45° F. (fig. 26).

By April 25, corn planting may begin in the southeast. Fifty-five degrees F. (13° C.) is a critical temperature for planting this important crop. Corn planting usually has spread to the southeastern third of the state by May 5. Grain sorghum and soybeans planting begins in the southeast about May 9, when the temperature averages 60° F. (16° C.). Corn planting is at its peak at this time and warm-season vegetables such as tomatoes, beans, cucumbers, and melons are planted in southeastern gardens.

RALPH E. NEILD

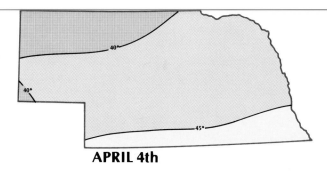

APRIL 4th

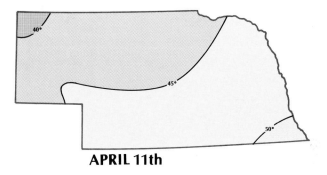

APRIL 11th

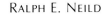
Fig. 26. MEAN DAILY SPRING TEMPERATURES

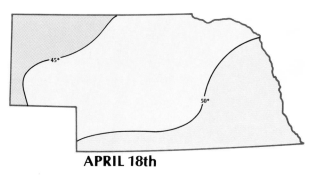

APRIL 18th

28

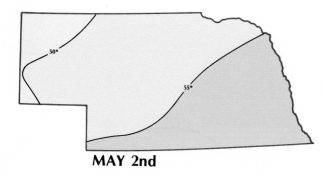

APRIL 25th

MAY 2nd

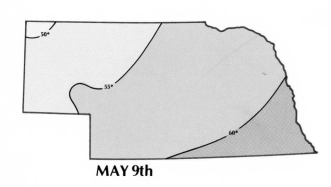

MAY 9th

THE FREEZE-FREE SEASON

There is a definite relationship between elevation, average freeze dates, and the freeze-free season. The average date of the last spring freeze is later, average date of the first fall freeze earlier, and freeze-free season shorter from east to west across the state. The warmest region in terms of length of freeze-free season is in the southeastern corner where the elevation averages about 1,000 feet (305 m.) above sea level. At higher elevations in the Panhandle (4,200 ft., or 1,280 m.) the last spring freeze is about four weeks later, the first fall freeze three weeks earlier, and freeze-free season seven weeks shorter (figs. 27–29).

Regions subject to cold air drainage along the river valleys and in much of the Sandhills show the effect of local topographic conditions that modify this general pattern. Urban "heat island" effects are noticed in and near larger towns, especially Omaha and Lincoln. Areas in the state that normally experience a freeze-free season of fewer than 120 days have recorded freezing temperatures during midsummer. Agate, a notoriously cold spot during the warm season, has registered a minimum of 29° F. (−2° C.) in mid-July.

The freeze-free season is often thought of as the growing season. It should be pointed out, however, that it is the crop's response to the entire temperature regime as well as average freeze data that determine growing-

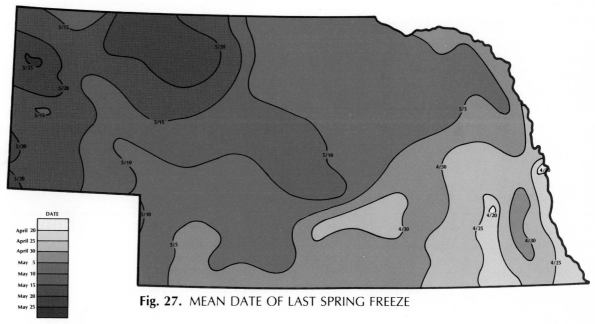

DATE

| April 20 |
| April 25 |
| April 30 |
| May 5 |
| May 10 |
| May 15 |
| May 20 |
| May 25 |

Fig. 27. MEAN DATE OF LAST SPRING FREEZE

29

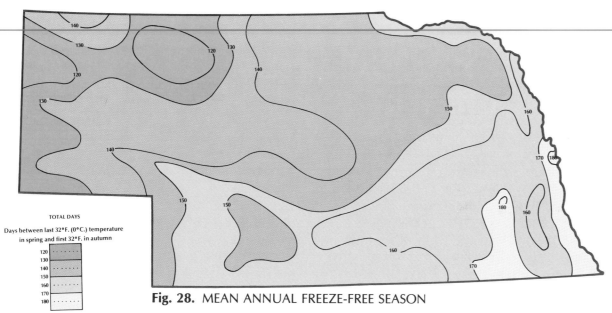

TOTAL DAYS

Days between last 32°F. (0°C.) temperature
in spring and first 32°F. in autumn

120	· · · · · ·
130	· · · · · ·
140	· · · · · ·
150	· · · · · ·
160	· · · · · ·
170	· · · · · ·
180	· · · · · ·

Fig. 28. MEAN ANNUAL FREEZE-FREE SEASON

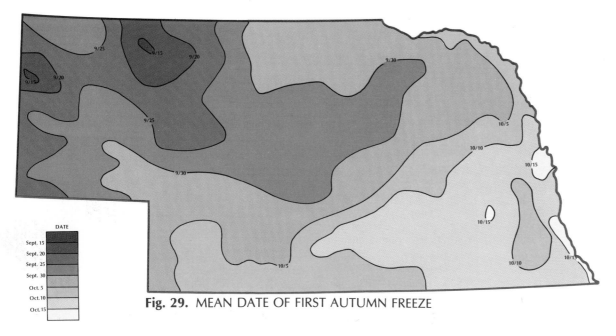

DATE

Sept. 15	
Sept. 20	
Sept. 25	
Sept. 30	
Oct. 5	
Oct. 10	
Oct. 15	

Fig. 29. MEAN DATE OF FIRST AUTUMN FREEZE

30

season length. Hardy cool-season crops such as small grains, sugar beets, and certain vegetables grow well even when they are subjected to light spring or fall freezes.

The possibility of an untimely late freeze after growth starts in the spring is of primary interest to farmers, gardeners, nurserymen, and other plant growers. Spring and the decreasing probability of freezing temperatures first enters southeastern Nebraska in April and progresses in a northwesterly direction across the state (figs. 30–33).

Plant species, stage of development, their condition, the intensity and duration of cold, and rate of thawing are factors that determine the severity of a freeze. For example, frosts may occur after spring temperatures become warm enough to induce seed germination and sustain early growth of crops such as corn. However, soil temperatures at shallow depths in the spring are usually warmer than the air temperature on days when a freeze occurs, so germinating seeds are not as vulnerable as seedlings after emergence. Frost at this time may damage corn leaves, but the growing point is below the soil and protected until plants are between 6 and 12 inches tall or taller. If frost occurs after that time, damage can be severe. The growing points of soybeans, dry edible beans, and alfalfa are above ground and are often damaged if the crops are planted too early.

An early autumn freeze before growth is completed is of concern to plant growers. Likewise, building contractors, automobile owners, and service station operators are among those whose operations and equipment may be affected by freezing weather.

Fig. 30. PROBABILITY OF SPRING FREEZE, APRIL 1

Early signs of autumn and the possibility of a freeze are first apparent in extreme northwestern Nebraska at the beginning of September (figs. 34–37). By October 15, there is a high probability that a freeze will have occurred over most of the state.

Tomatoes, corn, watermelon, zinnias, and other warm-season plants of tropical origin are damaged or destroyed by brief exposure to temperatures below 32° F. (0° C.). By contrast, winter wheat, apples, and tulips will not bloom or bear fruit unless growth is arrested by cold. Freeze damage to corn is slight if the kernels have a moisture content below 35 percent and will not be used for seed. Seed corn is not safe from temperature in the low 20s until kernel moisture is below 25 percent.

RALPH E. NEILD

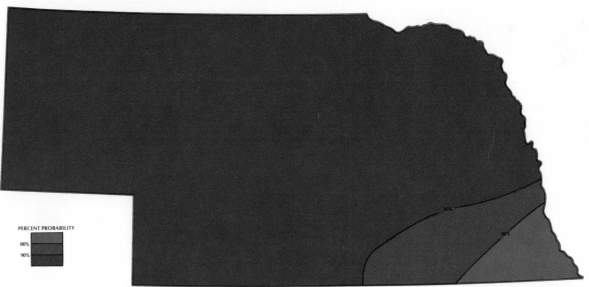

Fig. 31. PROBABILITY OF SPRING FREEZE, APRIL 15

31

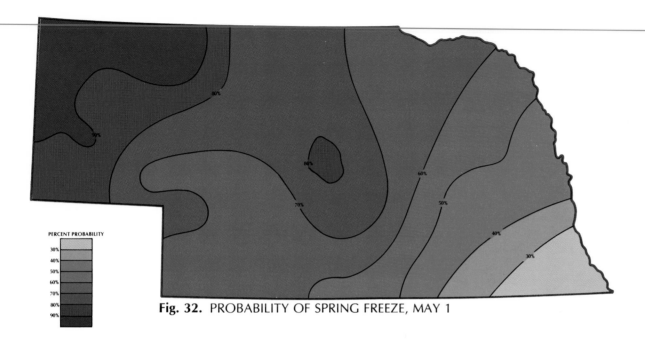

Fig. 32. PROBABILITY OF SPRING FREEZE, MAY 1

PERCENT PROBABILITY
30%
40%
50%
60%
70%
80%
90%

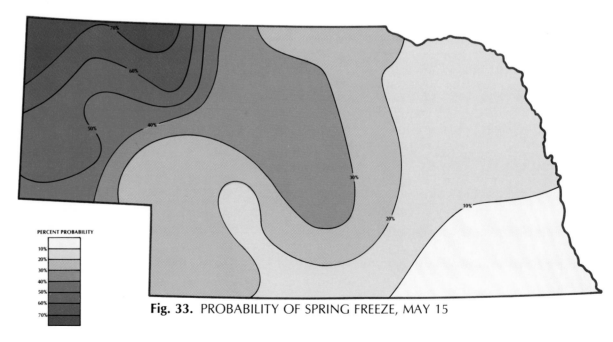

Fig. 33. PROBABILITY OF SPRING FREEZE, MAY 15

PERCENT PROBABILITY
10%
20%
30%
40%
50%
60%
70%

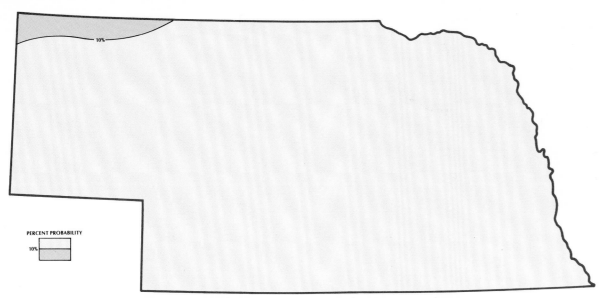

Fig. 34. PROBABILITY OF AUTUMN FREEZE, SEPTEMBER 1

PERCENT PROBABILITY

10%

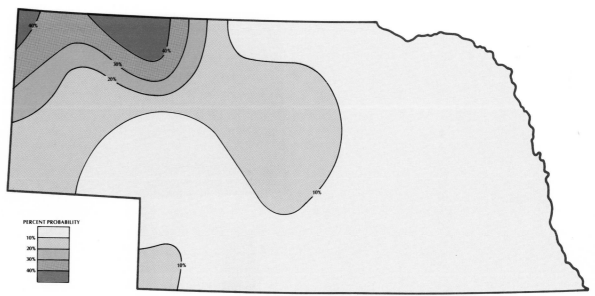

PERCENT PROBABILITY

10%
20%
30%
40%

Fig. 35. PROBABILITY OF AUTUMN FREEZE, SEPTEMBER 15

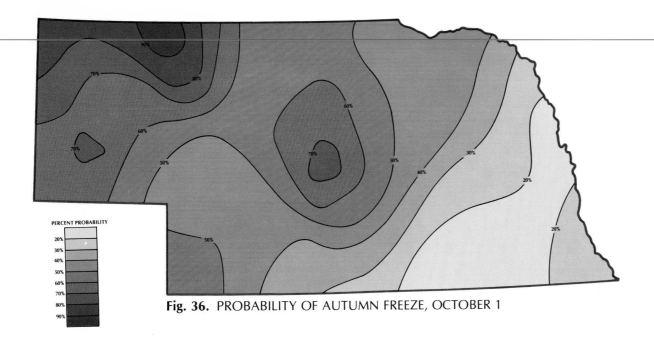

Fig. 36. PROBABILITY OF AUTUMN FREEZE, OCTOBER 1

PERCENT PROBABILITY

20%
30%
40%
50%
60%
70%
80%
90%

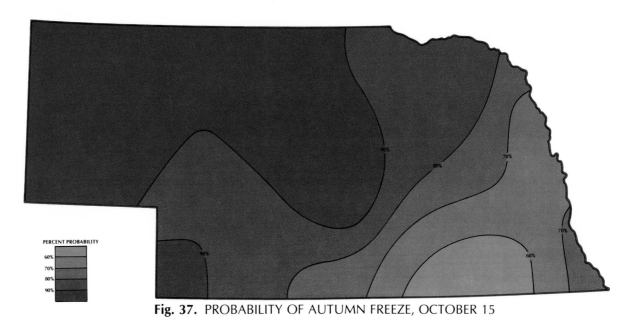

Fig. 37. PROBABILITY OF AUTUMN FREEZE, OCTOBER 15

PERCENT PROBABILITY

60%
70%
80%
90%

34

THE AGROCLIMATIC CALENDAR

Different crops require different temperature regimes. Each must be planted so that growth and development occur at the most favorable time for maximum yield and quality (graph 1). Cool-season crops such as wheat, oats, and onions germinate at a low temperature and tolerate frost, while warm-season crops like corn and beans may be injured at or below 32° F. (0° C.). With the exception of hardy fall-sown small grains and some forages that overwinter in a dormant condition, most Nebraska crops are planted in the spring, when temperature and precipitation are increasing.

The usual time of planting and harvesting operations in relation to freeze hazard and average temperature is diagramatically illustrated below. As may be seen, oat seeding begins when the average temperature first rises to 43° F. (6° C.), corn planting at 55° F. (13° C.), and bean planting at about 60° F. (16° C.).

Growing degree-days are a measure of the temperature requirements of crops. They are determined by subtracting a base temperature of 50° F. (10° C.) for warm-season crops like field corn, soybeans, and grain sorghum

Table 4. Base Temperatures and Growing Degree-Day Requirements for Various Crops

Crop	Base Temperature, Degrees F.	Total GDDs from Planting to Harvest
Peas	40	1,200–1,800
Barley	40	2,000–2,400
Spring Wheat	40	2,000–2,400
Oats	40	2,100–2,500
Snap Beans	50	1,100–1,550
Sweet Corn	50	1,750–2,000
Soybeans	50	2,000–2,400
Field Corn	50	2,200–3,000

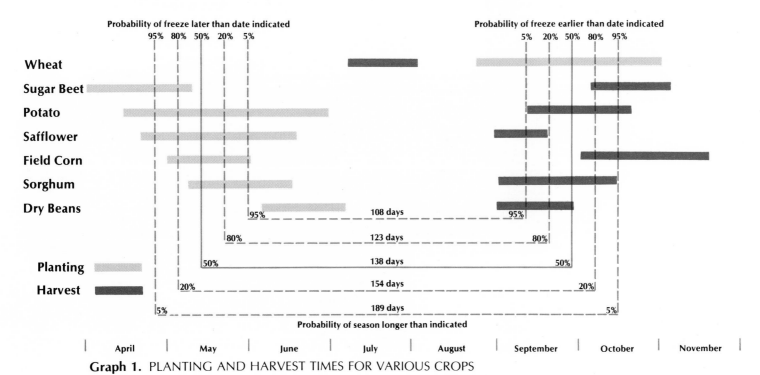

Graph 1. PLANTING AND HARVEST TIMES FOR VARIOUS CROPS

from the daily average temperature. These crops do not grow well below 50° F. Different crops and different varieties require certain accumulations of temperatures before they mature (table 4, figs. 38 and 39). Field corn hybrids adapted to cooler regions may require as few as 2,000 growing degree-days above 50° F. Hybrids adapted to warmer regions may require 3,000 or more growing degree-days.

The number of growing degree-days required for warm-season crops in Nebraska decreases from over 3,000 in the southeast to fewer than 2,000 in the northwest. It is obvious from the growing degree-day map why only short-season corn hybrids requiring fewer growing degree-days are adapted to western Nebraska and then may be harvested for silage instead of grain in years when temperatures and the number of growing degree-days are below normal.

RALPH E. NEILD

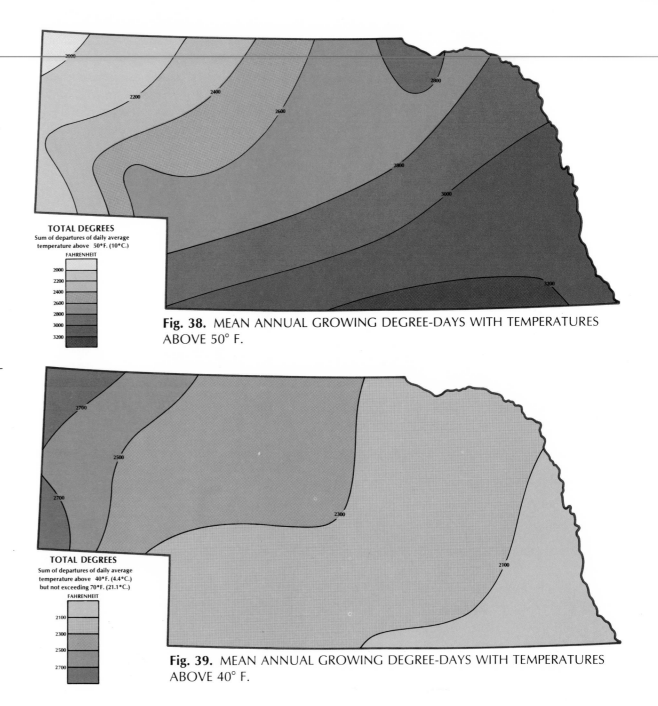

TOTAL DEGREES
Sum of departures of daily average temperature above 50° F. (10°C.)

FAHRENHEIT

2000
2200
2400
2600
2800
3000
3200

Fig. 38. MEAN ANNUAL GROWING DEGREE-DAYS WITH TEMPERATURES ABOVE 50° F.

TOTAL DEGREES
Sum of departures of daily average temperature above 40° F. (4.4°C.) but not exceeding 70°F. (21.1°C.)

FAHRENHEIT

2100
2300
2500
2700

Fig. 39. MEAN ANNUAL GROWING DEGREE-DAYS WITH TEMPERATURES ABOVE 40° F.

3
Atmospheric Humidity and Precipitation

Nebraska's Hydrologic Cycle
Humidity
Annual, Monthly, and Growing Season
    Precipitation
Precipitation Extremes
Thunderstorms, Lightning, and Hail
Climatic Aspects of Drought in Nebraska
Snowfall
Blizzards

NEBRASKA'S HYDROLOGIC CYCLE

The hydrologic, or water, cycle illustrates the exchange of water, in its various forms, over the earth's surface (fig. 40). It is a simple cycle when we consider only the ocean and the atmosphere. Moisture evaporates from the ocean, clouds form, and precipitation falling from the clouds returns the moisture back to the sea. The cycle becomes more complex, however, when we include consideration of the land surfaces. When the clouds move inland from the ocean, the precipitation falling on the land eventually returns to the sea, but this journey can become quite involved.

Precipitation can be stored on the land in the form of ice or snow, on the surfaces of many forms of vegetation, or in the soil or lakes and ponds. Ultimately the ice and snow melt, sending their runoff back to the sea, and water stored in the soil in time reaches the sea either by joining the surface runoff or by the slow journey beneath the surface to the oceans.

The cycle is complicated even further when we consider that a certain portion of the precipitation collected by the land and vegetation is evaporated (from free-standing water), released by plants by means of transpiration, and sublimated (evaporated directly from ice and snow without melting),

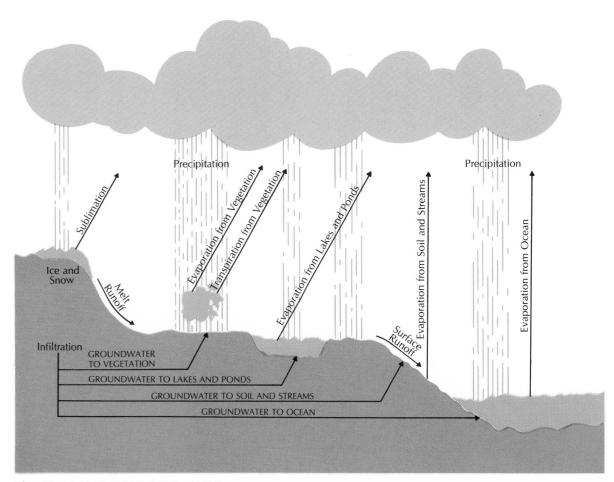

Fig. 40. THE HYDROLOGIC CYCLE

38

resulting in the formation of more clouds and precipitation.

Although we think of the cycle as being completed when the moisture which left the oceans has returned via the atmosphere and land, the hydrologic cycle in fact has no beginning or end. The waters of the twentieth century are the waters of geologic history; the same water has been transferred time and time again from the oceans into the atmosphere, dropped upon the land, and transferred back to the sea. The only variation has been in the magnitude of the individual components. There have been times in the past when the amount of water stored in ice and snow was far greater than it is today. Large-scale droughts have occurred, reducing the amount of water received as precipitation. Even though these are dramatic changes in the components of the cycle, however, they are related to a changing climate and not to the amount of water in the entire hydrologic cycle.

·A great deal of mental and physical effort has been expended in an attempt to alter various components of the hydrologic cycle on a regional basis to man's advantage. The conservation of water resources (the building of a storage reservoir on a stream, for example) is intimately related to one or more of the phases in the hydrologic cycle. Rain making (cloud seeding) does not increase the amount of water in the hydrologic cycle, but it may speed up the precipitation portion of the cycle so that more water is available at a given time and place for immediate use. Undoubtably, the ma-

nipulation of the hydrologic cycle on a local or regional basis will become an economic and social issue much debated between those who feel that it is important not to alter a naturally functioning system and those who feel that the system can and should be altered to meet the needs of man.

The significance of the hydrologic cycle becomes apparent when we examine Nebraska's portion of it to see how much water is made available for various purposes. The first step is to determine the "local water budget" across the state. Graph 2 presents a simplified version of the local water budget in table and graph form for western, central, and eastern Nebraska locations. P stands for monthly amounts of precipitation and PE for the potential (or possible) evapotranspiration—the evaporation of free-standing water and the transpiration of moisture from the soil through vegetation. PE can be thought of as the average monthly demand for moisture by the natural environment. Subtracting the demand for precipitation from the actual precipitation (P−PE) shows by what amount precipitation exceeds or falls short of the environmental demand at different times of the year.

As illustrated in graph 2, PE reaches a maximum at all three locations in summer (when temperatures are at their highest and moisture demand the greatest) and a minimum in the winter (when there is very little demand for moisture because of the low temperatures). In all areas of the state the amount of precipitation received from November through late April and early May ex-

ceeds the environmental demand. Although it is the time of year when the state normally receives its smallest monthly amounts of precipitation, that precipitation which does fall is utilized to recharge soil moisture and increase the amount of water stored in reservoirs across the state.

From mid-May through October the demand for moisture is not met by the monthly precipitation. Therefore, the moisture stored in the soil during the earlier part of the year must be drawn upon and utilized in addition to the precipitation received during this period for the growth of vegetation. As graph 2 shows, the difference between the demand for moisture and the actual precipitation becomes greater from east to west across the state. On an annual basis Omaha is .82 inch (21 mm.), Grand Island 3.78 inches (96 mm.), and Scottsbluff 10.19 inches (259 mm.) short of the demand for moisture. Hence, as we proceed westward through the state, dryland farming, relying on precipitation and stored soil moisture, becomes increasingly risky. Fortunately, water is accessible in another portion of the hydrologic cycle: the streams and rivers passing through the state and the aquifers, or layers of water-bearing rock, beneath the surface of the soil. Drawing upon these sources for irrigation provides adequate water for agricultural needs, but raises the question of whether there is a danger of lowering the water table (and causing it to rise in other locations).

One of the striking features of the Nebraska's hydrologic cycle is the seasonal timing

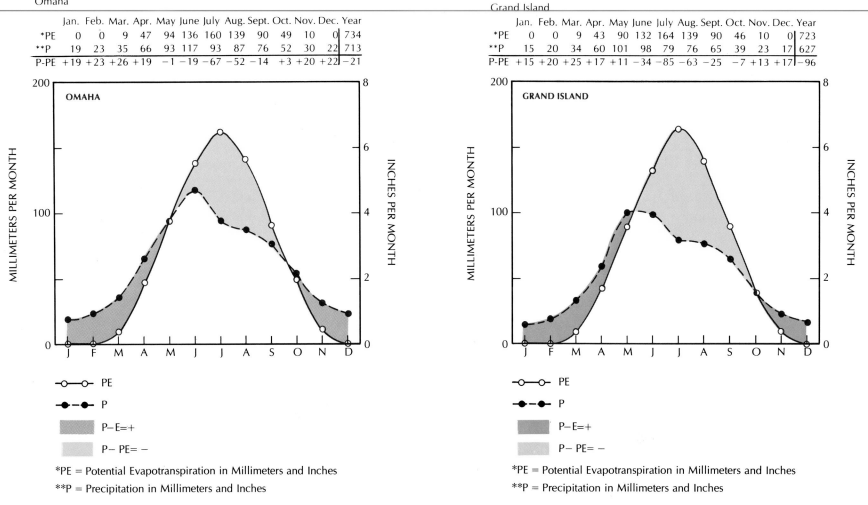

Omaha

	Jan.	Feb.	Mar.	Apr.	May	June	July	Aug.	Sept.	Oct.	Nov.	Dec.	Year
*PE	0	0	9	47	94	136	160	139	90	49	10	0	734
**P	19	23	35	66	93	117	93	87	76	52	30	22	713
P-PE	+19	+23	+26	+19	−1	−19	−67	−52	−14	+3	+20	+22	−21

Grand Island

	Jan.	Feb.	Mar.	Apr.	May	June	July	Aug.	Sept.	Oct.	Nov.	Dec.	Year
*PE	0	0	9	43	90	132	164	139	90	46	10	0	723
**P	15	20	34	60	101	98	79	76	65	39	23	17	627
P-PE	+15	+20	+25	+17	+11	−34	−85	−63	−25	−7	+13	+17	−96

PE
P
P−E=+
P−PE=−

*PE = Potential Evapotranspiration in Millimeters and Inches
**P = Precipitation in Millimeters and Inches

*PE = Potential Evapotranspiration in Millimeters and Inches
**P = Precipitation in Millimeters and Inches

Graph 2. THE LOCAL WATER BUDGET (data from ''Average Climatic Water Balance Data of the Continents,'' *Publications in Climatology*, vol. 17, no. 3 [1964])

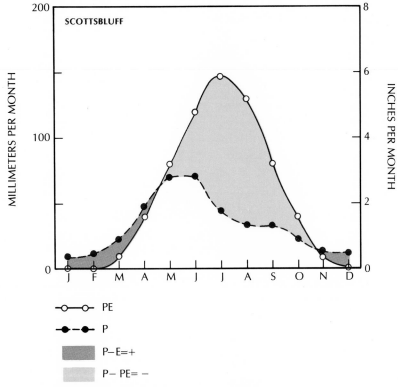

Scottsbluff

	Jan.	Feb.	Mar.	Apr.	May	June	July	Aug.	Sept.	Oct.	Nov.	Dec.	Year
*PE	0	0	9	40	79	118	146	129	81	40	7	0	649
**P	−9	12	22	47	70	70	45	34	34	23	12	12	390
P-PE	+9	+12	+13	+7	−9	−48	−101	−95	−47	−17	+5	+12	−259

—o—o— PE

—●—●— P

P−E=+

P− PE= −

*PE = Potential Evapotranspiration in Millimeters
**P   = Precipitation in Millimeters

of precipitation. One can speculate what type of climate the state would have if the seasonal distribution were reversed. With a winter rather than a summer maximum of precipitation, much of the precipitation would fall as heavy snow on frozen ground and would melt and run off rapidly in the spring. If there were little precipitation in the summer and the demand for moisture remained at its present level, Nebraska's summer environment would be a desert. The amount of irrigation would have to be increased greatly to support a significant level of agricultural production. Therefore, although the state's precipitation often takes the form of heavy (sometimes damaging) late spring and summer thunderstorms, it is fortunate that most of the precipitation falls during the growing season.

KENNETH F. DEWEY

HUMIDITY

"It's not the heat so much as the humidity," Nebraskans seem to echo across the state during the hot summer months. Human body temperature is affected by the evaporative loss of moisture from the surface of the skin. The rate of evaporation, which decreases as the relative humidity of the air increases, determines the body's sensible temperature. When the humidity and air temperature are high, people really "feel" the heat.

Cities generally have a lower relative humidity than rural areas, probably because there are fewer plants transpiring water vapor, precipitation is removed rapidly through storm sewers, and streets and buildings retain heat, causing higher temperatures.

Relative humidity measurements are recorded only at first order weather stations in Nebraska. Graph 3 reveals the variation in relative humidity across the state on a monthly basis at 6:00 a.m. and noon. There appears to be little seasonal variation in morning readings. September mornings generally average above 80 percent relative humidity, but the annual range is less than 10 percent. Because temperatures are higher at midday, noon humidity recordings are lower, especially during summer months. As expected, afternoon relative humidities decline slightly from east to west across Nebraska.

MERLIN P. LAWSON

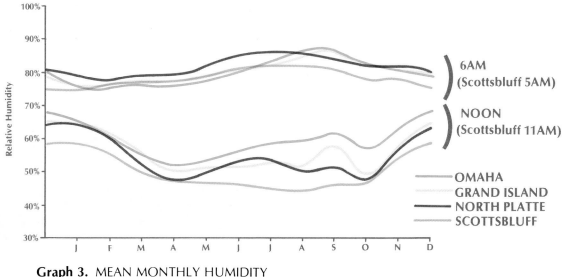

Graph 3. MEAN MONTHLY HUMIDITY

ANNUAL, MONTHLY, AND GROWING SEASON PRECIPITATION

The average annual precipitation in Nebraska ranges from less than 15 inches (381 mm.) in the Panhandle to more than 36 inches (914 mm.) in the southeastern corner of the state (fig. 41). The decrease in precipitation toward the west and north reflects the increasing distance of those areas from Nebraska's primary source of moisture, the Gulf of Mexico.

One of the characteristic features of Nebraska's precipitation is its uneven seasonal distribution: January has the least and June the most (fig. 42). In fact, almost 80 percent of the state's precipitation falls as rain during the six-month period April through September. This growing season precipitation ranges from less than 15 inches (381 mm.) in the western one-third of the state to more than 23 inches (584 mm.) in the southeastern area (fig. 43). During all months of the year the pattern of precipitation across the state remains similar to the annual pattern, decreasing from east to west. The annual number of days with precipitation of one-half inch or more also decreases toward the western portion of the state. Southeastern Nebraska averages over twenty-two such days and the Panhandle less than ten (fig. 44).

KENNETH F. DEWEY

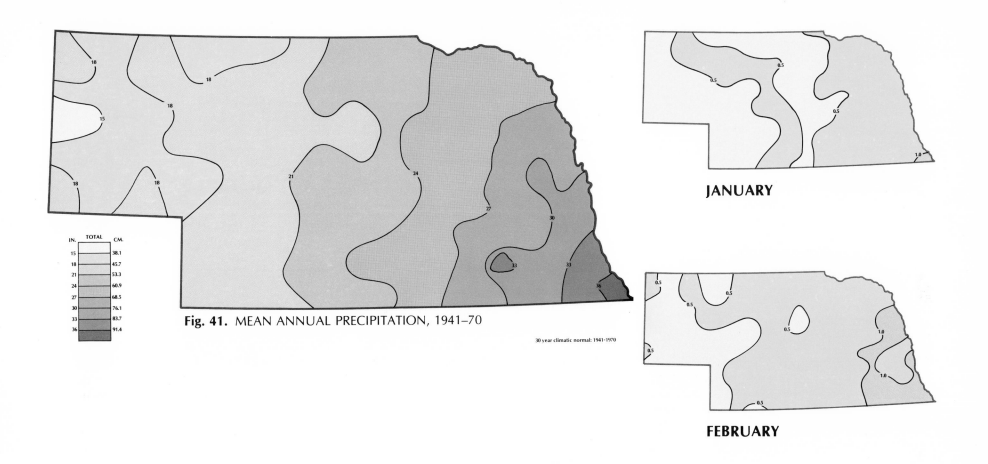

Fig. 41. MEAN ANNUAL PRECIPITATION, 1941–70

IN.	TOTAL	CM.
15		38.1
18		45.7
21		53.3
24		60.9
27		68.5
30		76.1
33		83.7
36		91.4

30 year climatic normal: 1941-1970

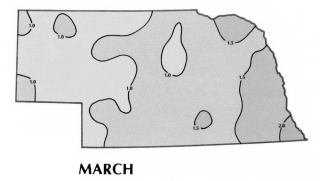

JANUARY

FEBRUARY

Fig. 42. MEAN MONTHLY PRECIPITATION, 1941–70

MARCH

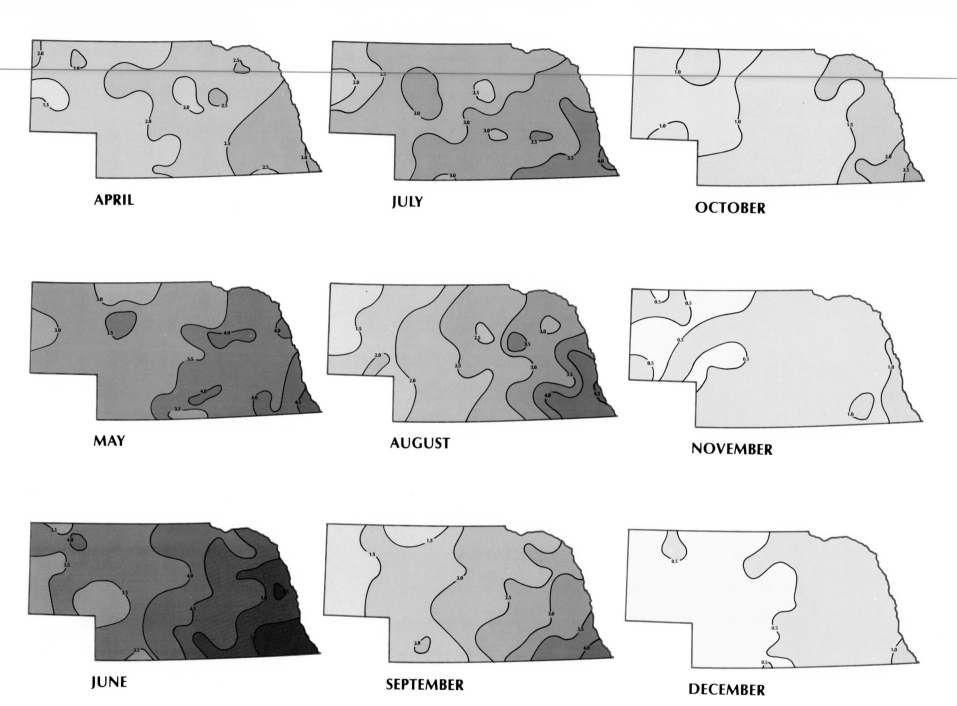

APRIL

JULY

OCTOBER

MAY

AUGUST

NOVEMBER

JUNE

SEPTEMBER

DECEMBER

44

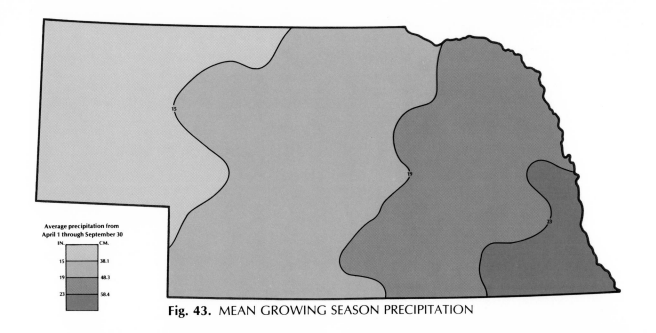

**Average precipitation from
April 1 through September 30**

IN.		CM.
15		38.1
19		48.3
23		58.4

Fig. 43. MEAN GROWING SEASON PRECIPITATION

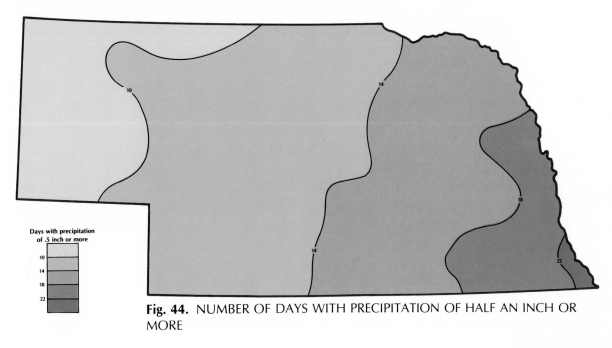

**Days with precipitation
of .5 inch or more**

10
14
18
22

Fig. 44. NUMBER OF DAYS WITH PRECIPITATION OF HALF AN INCH OR
MORE

PRECIPITATION EXTREMES

One of the most significant features of Nebraska's precipitation pattern is the high variability in precipitation amounts from year to year and from season to season, due largely to the continentality of the state.

Since the primary source of Nebraska's moisture is the Gulf of Mexico and the flow of Gulf air into the state requires southeasterly winds across the lower Mississippi valley and the eastern Great Plains, the frequency of southeasterly air streams is related to the amount of precipitation received across the state. An examination of one-hundred years' weather records for Omaha shows that 45.74 inches (1,162 mm.) of precipitation fell during 1881, a year of frequent summer southeasterly winds, while only 14.90 inches (378 mm.) fell during 1934, a year of frequent southwesterly winds and infrequent incursions of Gulf air masses.

If we examine the seasonal variability in precipitation amounts, the most intense precipitation occurs with late spring and summer convective thunderstorms (which are caused by heated air rising from the earth's surface and cooling to the dew point temperature so that precipitation occurs). At that time of year temperatures are quite warm and the amount of water that the air can hold for the occurrence of precipitation is at a maximum (as the air warms, the amount of water that can be transported also increases). The potential for heavy rainfalls is correspondingly at a maximum during this time of year. Fortunately, intense convective rainfalls are usually local phenomena and cover only small areas.

Occasionally, heavy rainfalls will result in the issuance by the National Weather Service of flash flood warnings for low-lying areas, although much of the damage formerly caused by heavy rains has been reduced by conservation and flood-control projects. In order to develop a flood-control system, it is essential to know the probability of heavy rainfall, which is derived by a mathematical extension of actual observations.

The expected maximum one-hour rainfall for a one-year period is theoretically similar to the average of the observed annual one-hour maxima for weather stations across the state (fig. 45). Southeastern Nebraska should average one rainfall a year with an accumulation of almost 1.5 inches (38.1 mm.) in one hour. In the Panhandle the normal value is less than 1 inch (25.4 mm.). Similarly, the expected maximum accumulation for a twenty-four-hour period during one year decreases to the west (fig. 46).

The anticipated one-hour precipitation maximum that should recur only once in one hundred years is almost 4 inches (101.6 mm.) in the southeast (fig. 47). This type of information is important for engineering the removal of storm waters, especially in urban centers. Precipitation maxima may exceed these calculated values, but the probable occurrence would be less than once in one hundred years. The largest twenty-four-hour rainfall recorded in the state—13.15 inches (334 mm.)—occurred on July 8 and 9, 1950, at York.

KENNETH F. DEWEY
MERLIN P. LAWSON

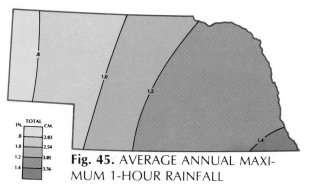

IN.	TOTAL	CM.
.8		2.03
1.0		2.54
1.2		3.05
1.4		3.56

Fig. 45. AVERAGE ANNUAL MAXIMUM 1-HOUR RAINFALL

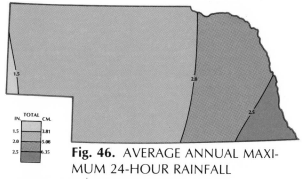

IN.	TOTAL	CM.
1.5		3.81
2.0		5.08
2.5		6.35

Fig. 46. AVERAGE ANNUAL MAXIMUM 24-HOUR RAINFALL

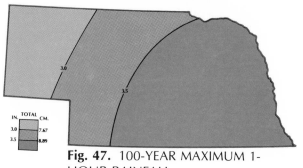

IN.	TOTAL	CM.
3.0		7.67
3.5		8.89

Fig. 47. 100-YEAR MAXIMUM 1-HOUR RAINFALL

THUNDERSTORMS, LIGHTNING, AND HAIL

Thunderstorms are an integral part of life on the prairie-plains of Nebraska. Although few areas in the United States are free from their spectacular display of lightning, Nebraska residents experience thunderstorms an average of fifty days during the summer (fig. 48). The attendant cloudbursts account for over 70 percent of the state's total annual precipitation.

For those working in city office buildings or driving tractors in the field, the storms are first announced by a familiar crackling on the radio. Soon it turns ominously dark as clouds towering more than 40,000 feet into the stratosphere slowly obliterate the mid-afternoon sunshine. Cars with headlights and windshield wipers in operation alert farmers to leave their fields for chores that can be accomplished in the safety of their barns. Country school yards become deserted, their emptied swings continuing to sway in the gusty, cold wind. Suddenly the dull gray landscape is illuminated as a flash descends from the base of the swirling cloud. A deep, thundering roar barrels across the countryside, its vibrations felt as much as heard. The swirling dust is almost instantly replaced by a sheet of water, huge droplets that because of the driving wind can no longer be discerned as individual drops. In spite of the fury of these spectacular storms, Nebraskans in city and coun-

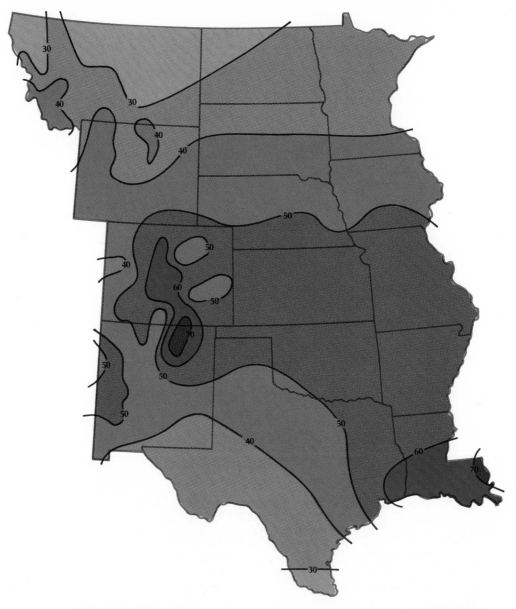

Fig. 48. MEAN ANNUAL NUMBER OF DAYS WITH THUNDERSTORMS (from John L. Baldwin, *Climates of the United States* [Environmental Data Service, National Oceanic and Atmospheric Administration, 1973])

try alike welcome the life-giving moisture and temporary relief from summer heat that accompany them.

The generation of a thunderstorm is associated with what weathermen describe as thermal instability in the atmosphere. This convective instability, or buoyancy of the air, results when unequal heating or cooling occurs in the land-air interface, causing a vertical upward motion in the atmosphere. The intensity of the storm is determined by the degree of instability. Nebraska's high surface temperatures provide a favorable environment for initiating updrafts. Other triggering mechanisms include radiational cooling of cloud tops, the gliding of one air mass over another, and the lifting of warm, moist air over hills and mountains.

Thunderstorms appear to evolve through certain phases as they build, mature, and decline in intensity. At first, an updraft of buoyant warm, moist air creates a convective cell. As the air rises, it cools until the moisture in it condenses, forming large vertical masses of clouds. The updrafts are surrounded by higher atmospheric pressure which leads to continued convergence of surface winds bringing additional atmospheric moisture as they too rise. This water vapor represents an additional source of heat energy for the weather machine. As it

Time-lapse photo of lightning strokes associated with a thunderstorm in southeast Lincoln. (Photo by Gary Smith)

48

condenses from a gas into droplets of water, energy that was consumed during initial evaporation is released to the atmosphere. This energy had been effectively stored until condensation resulted in its release.

As the cloud grows in mass, water droplets and/or ice particles grow large enough to fall within the convective cloud. The cloud tower continues to rise to an altitude where only wispy particles of ice exist. Now the thunderstorm measures several miles across at its base and looms to seven or more miles in height. High-level winds sheer the cloud top so that it has the appearance of an anvil.

The thunderstorm reaches maturity when precipitation particles are large enough to fall from the convective cells. The rainfall pattern within a thunderstorm is closely related to the distribution and stage of cell development. The duration of heavy rain also varies with the cell size, ranging from minutes in small, weak cells to as much as an hour in large, active cells. The friction of falling rain attended by evaporative cooling eventually initiates downdrafts of air.

During the complex energy exchanges occurring within the growing thundercloud, a large electrical field is generated. Although there is no completely acceptable theory to explain the process of electrification during thunderstorm activity, there appears to be an important relationship between the formation of precipitation particles and lightning.

It is known, however, that the normal distribution of electricity in a thundercloud is positively charged particles in the upper region and negatively charged particles near the cloud base. The earth normally maintains a negative charge, but as the thunderstorm passes over, it induces a "shadow" of positive charge on the ground below. During fair weather there is a normal flow of electrical current from the atmosphere to the ground. The lightning associated with thunderstorms appears to reverse this flow. Around the world approximately one-hundred strokes of lightning occur per second.

Lightning is the discharge between positive and negative electrical potential through the atmosphere from cloud to cloud, cloud to ground, or ground to cloud. The light produced by a stroke of lightning results from the intense heat of 18,000° F., which causes the air molecules to glow. Thunder is the sound produced by the vigorous expanson of this heated air.

During this mature stage of the thunderstorm, lightning, rain, wind, hail, and even tornadoes seem to reach maximum intensity. But eventually the downdrafts of gusty cold wind interfere with the storm-sustaining updrafts which contain the necessary sources of moisture and heat energy, and the thunderstorm soon dissipates.

Occasionally hail, perhaps the most destructive form of precipitation, falls from the base of these convective clouds. Hailstones are most commonly pea-sized but can grow to over four inches in diameter. These large stones have a cross section, similar to that of an onion, in which concentric shells of alternating clear and "frosted" ice have been formed. They are generated within violent updrafts which carry supercooled water droplets and ice particles up and down through repeated cycles of melting and freezing (fig. 49). Once the weight of the hailstone exceeds the force of an updraft or becomes swept into a downdraft, it falls to earth. Thus, the path of hail destruction is confined to narrow belts within individual storms. The size of the path is dependent on the velocity and life of the storm cell, and the intensity of hail varies considerably within short distances. In Nebraska, hailstorms tend to move in a northeasterly direction.

Hailstorms in the state usually begin in April, are most frequent in June, and cease by the end of September. The highest proportion of hailstorms occur in the Panhandle, where 10 percent of the thunderstorms produce hail (fig. 50). The percentage is much smaller to the east. Although most thunderstorms occur during the summer, spring storms are more likely to be accompanied by hail. During April, one storm in five in the Panhandle has hail.

Afternoon and evening hours between three o'clock and nine o'clock have the greatest incidence of hail damage. It is fortunate that these dramatic storms are of short duration: a study conducted close to the Colorado-Nebraska border revealed that one-third of the hailstorms lasted less than five minutes and 80 percent lasted less than fifteen minutes.

Property and crop losses caused by hail are tremendous in the United States. Hail

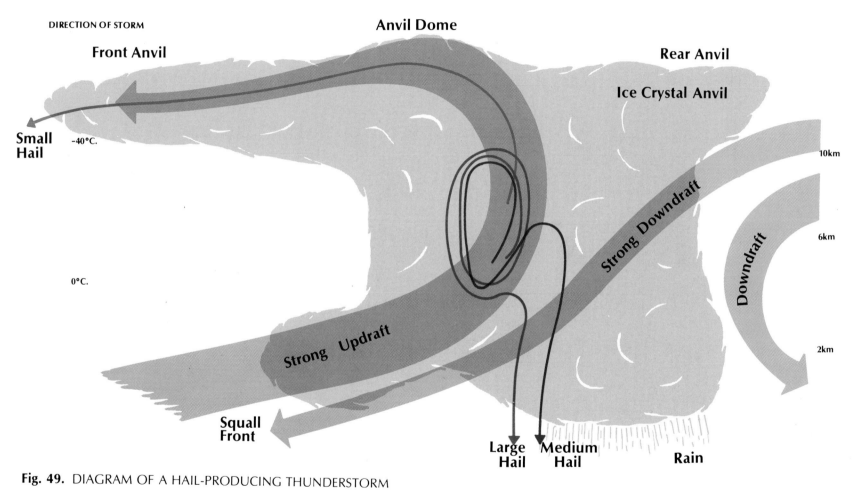

DIRECTION OF STORM

Front Anvil

Anvil Dome

Rear Anvil

Ice Crystal Anvil

Small
Hail

−40°C.

10km

6km

Strong Downdraft

0°C.

Downdraft

2km

Strong Updraft

Squall
Front

Large
Hail

Medium
Hail

Rain

Fig. 49. DIAGRAM OF A HAIL-PRODUCING THUNDERSTORM

50

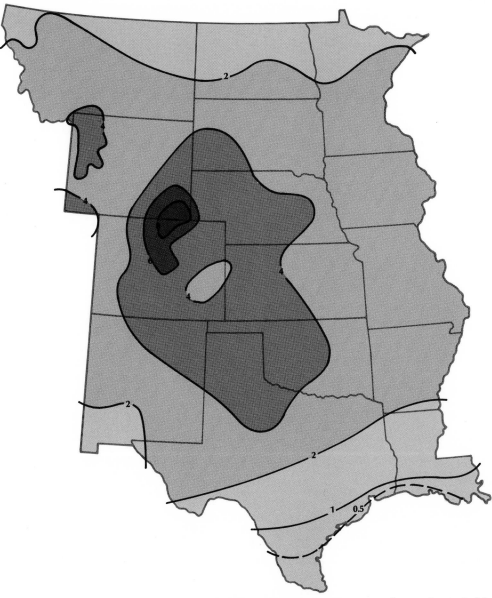

Fig. 50. MEAN ANNUAL NUMBER OF DAYS WITH HAIL (from John L. Baldwin, *Climates of the United States* [Environmental Data Service, National Oceanic and Atmospheric Administration, 1973])

insurance on crops costs Great Plains farmers well over $100 million annually. Losses estimated at $5 million resulted in southwestern Nebraska when hailstones up to half an inch in diameter cut a swath four to eight miles wide and two-hundred miles long through wheat and corn on June 18, 1970.

The Nebraska Panhandle (Kimball County, in particular) lies in an area having the highest incidence of hail in the United States. This region has a reputation for suffering from hail damage because wheat, the principal crop, has headed and therefore is most vulnerable to damage during the period of greatest hail frequency.

Plants have a remarkable ability to recuperate from hail injury if not damaged too extensively or at a critical stage of development. For example, early in the season, the growing point of some crops such as wheat, corn, and grain sorghum is below the surface of the soil and therefore is not vulnerable to hail. Recovery is rapid at this time even though above-ground damage is severe. In beans, however, the growing point rises above ground with the emerging seedling. These plants are capable of generating new foliage if the stem is not severed or too badly bruised. Root crops such as beets and potatoes are able to regenerate themselves, particularly if damage occurs at an early stage of growth, although damage to potatoes when they are twelve to fifteen inches tall and in bloom is critical.

MERLIN P. LAWSON

CLIMATIC ASPECTS OF DROUGHT IN NEBRASKA

Throughout the twentieth century climatologists have considered the Great Plains to be highly susceptible to large fluctuations in precipitation. In marginal regions of sub-humid rainfall (i.e., in areas where the long-term moisture supply approximates the potential evapotranspiration) it is possible for either abnormally wet or unusually dry conditions to persist for a number of years.

During drought years, ground water and water stored in reservoirs and lakes is of critical importance to agriculture. Nebraska has over 19 million acres of land suitable for irrigation with present technology, and approximately 2 billion acre-feet of ground water stored in its unique aquifer systems. Although only 6.2 million acres are currently irrigated, approximately 40 percent of the total value of crops is produced on irrigated land. With its vast potential water resources, the state is less vulnerable to rainfall deficiency, but its economic success is delicately aligned to the effective utilization, control, and conservation of water during periods of drought.

Historical weather records demonstrate that drought in Nebraska and other portions of the North American grasslands is a normal recurring phenomenon. Meterological measurements were not recorded in Nebraska until 1849, when the army surgeon at Fort Kearny was instructed to make such observations. Fort Kearny was one of twelve forts in the trans-Mississippi West at which weather records were kept and presented in reports concerned with sickness and mortality among army personnel (fig. 51).

By supplementing these widely dispersed meteorological observations with comments on the weather in diaries, letters, and published works, the late N. A. Bengston, a geographer at the University of Nebraska, summarized average annual precipitation in Nebraska back to 1850 (graph 4). The record shows that precipitation has been extremely variable (fig. 52).

There is no question that the state's settlers have had to endure alternate periods of drought and abundant rainfall, although during times of adequate rainfall people tend to forget that drought is a normal condition in a region, like Nebraska, of marginal climatic character. The extreme variability of annual precipitation in Nebraska can be demonstrated by lines connecting points of equal precipitation (isohyets) during two years. In 1915 the state experienced more rainfall than in any other year of modern record. The 30-inch (760-mm.) isohyet bisected the Sandhills and then was diverted westward into northeastern Colorado. By contrast, the dry conditions of the 1930s are signified by the radical eastward deflection of isohyets. More than two-thirds of the state received less than 15 inches (380 mm.) of precipitation in 1934.

Dust storm at Alma, Nebraska, in the 1930s. (Photo courtesy of the Nebraska State Historical Society)

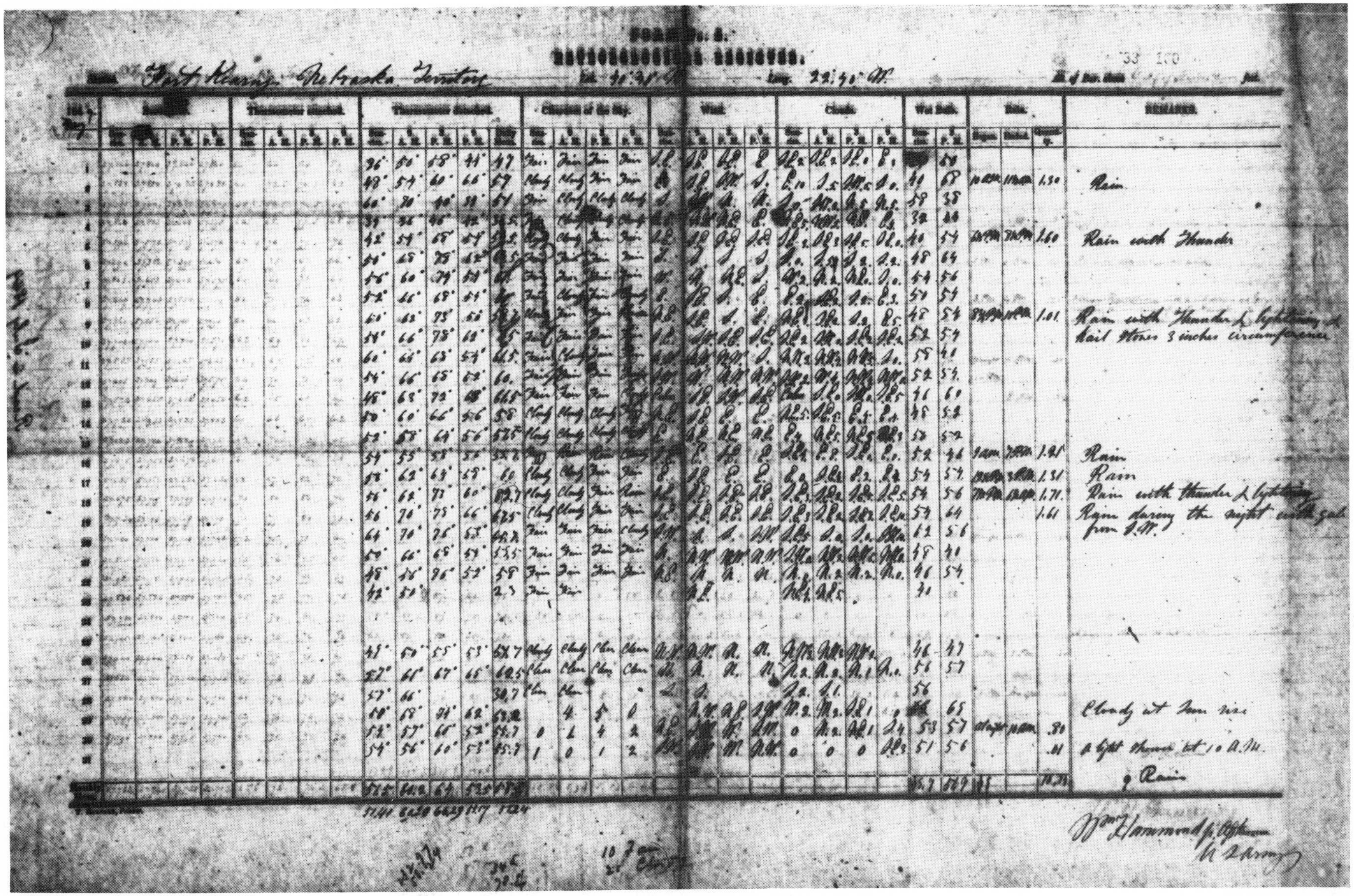

Fig. 51. FORT KEARNY METEOROLOGICAL JOURNAL. Post surgeons recorded their observations by the month on forms similar to the one above for June 1849.

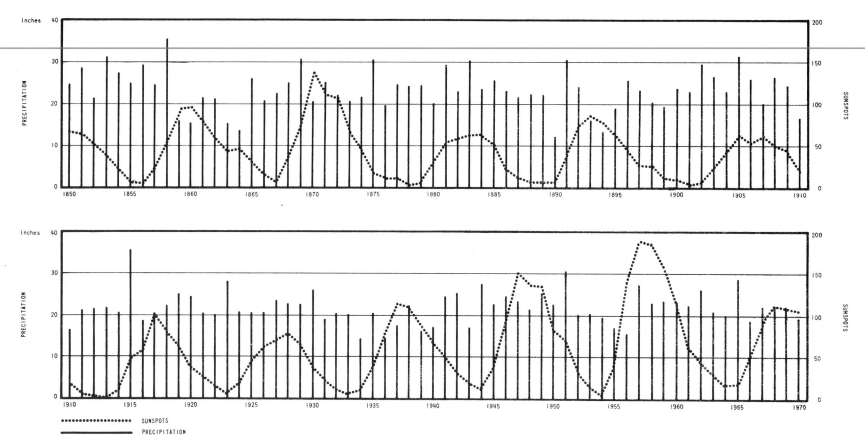

Graph 4. CORRESPONDENCE OF AVERAGE ANNUAL PRECIPITATION AND SOLAR ACTIVITY IN NEBRASKA, 1850–1970

Drought of the 1890s

The first drought following statehood began suddenly in 1890 with one of the driest years of the modern meteorological record. The following two years brought considerably more moisture, but the summers of '93 and '94 left fields parched. This dry spell was statewide, but the south-central and southwestern counties were most severely affected. In these areas, thousands of farms were abandoned and later sold for back taxes. People were badly prepared for such a harsh drought, and even in the wetter year of 1895 recovery was extremely slow. Many people left the plains, never to return. Others, however, did return to rebuild and prepare for future droughts with the painful experience of climatic extremes on the Great Plains burned into their memories.

Before this drought, Nebraska farmers depended largely on farming methods imported from the humid east. They tended to judge the agricultural value of the land simply by its superficial features, not by the nature of the soil, climate, or water supply. Some of the land should never have been plowed.

Immediately following the drought of the 1890s, dry-farming techniques increased throughout the Great Plains and were proclaimed the ultimate solution to drought problems. As a result, there was a renewed wave of settlement in this area during the early 1900s.

54

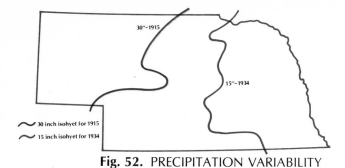

Fig. 52. PRECIPITATION VARIABILITY

30″-1915

15″-1934

~ 30 inch isohyet for 1915
~ 15 inch isohyet for 1934

Local Droughts of the Teens

The drought of 1893–95 was followed by a thirty-five-year period of normal to near-normal precipitation except for one rather dry year, 1910, and one excessively wet year, 1915. Local drought conditions were experienced from 1910 to 1915, after which normality was the rule until 1931. The most favorable decade in the United States from the beginning of weather records up to 1947 was from 1905 to 1915, when annual rainfall averaged 30 inches (760 mm.).

Drought of the 1930s

Chronic droughts began in 1931, culminating with the "dust bowl" conditions as the desert appeared to be spreading from the Southwest into the plains. In 1930 a widespread drought, which was to last for a decade, began east of the Rockies. The "dusters" and "black blizzards" which characterized this time of crop failure were a part of the national rainfall deficiency from 1930 to 1939. In 1936 it was esti-

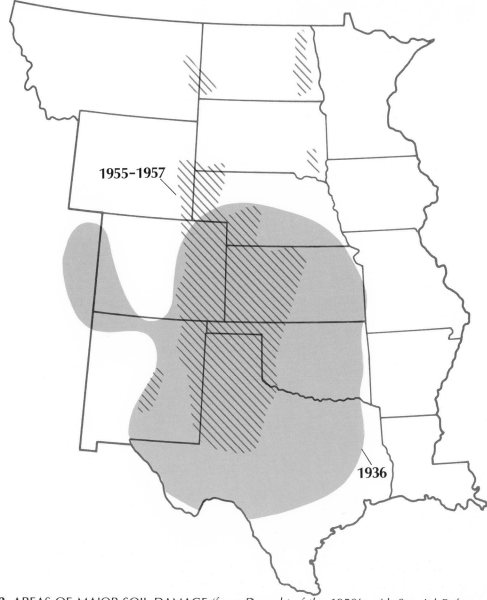

1955-1957

1936

Fig. 53. AREAS OF MAJOR SOIL DAMAGE (from *Drought of the 1950's with Special Reference to the Midcontinent*, United States Geological Survey Water-Supply Paper 1804 [1965]). With soil moisture depleted and vegetation dead or overgrazed, the dry, loose soils of the plains were subject to severe wind erosion. Strong winter winds and the lack of precipitation led to the removal of most of the soil during the "blow season" from November to May.

mated that 165,000 people, or approximately 40,000 families, had moved out of the Great Plains drought area since 1930. At its greatest extent, the "dust bowl" covered some 50 million acres on the Great Plains (fig. 53). By 1939 it had shrunk to about 10 million acres, but a shortage of rainfall in that year revived the dust storms. Greater rainfall in succeeding years finally brought the plains back to a nearly normal climatological state.

Drought of the 1950s

In the 1950s the United States experienced still another extended period of drought in which the same types of detrimental effects were felt, although the population was better prepared to combat dry conditions than in the 1890s and 1930s. In the Southwest and the southern Great Plains, the drought of the 1950s was one of the most severe on record; however, conditions in Nebraska were less severe than those experienced in the two preceding drought periods. Still, some people within the most affected areas suffered great financial loss and personal hardship. Below-normal precipitation from 1952 to 1957 caused critical water shortages in a major portion of the southern half of the nation.

Because of increasing municipal and industrial demands on water, future drought conditions will affect many more activities. A severe drought today, therefore, has a more widespread potential impact upon our civilization. Dry conditions may be amplified by other causes of water shortage such as overexploitation of water reserves, lack of storage and distribution facilities, improper design of distribution facilities, poor management of water supplies and watersheds, and increasing demands for water from industry and the population in general. In fact, these conditions can cause a depletion of the water supply even during humid climatic conditions.

Drought of the '70s?

Of critical concern to the citizens of Nebraska is the question of recurrence of drought in the state. Many investigators have suggested that the major droughts in the central plains have occurred at distinct intervals of approximately twenty-two years. Few scientists would disagree that dry conditions in the West and Middle West are associated with contemporaneous shifts in the general atmospheric circulation of the globe. Severe disagreement exists about the basic cause of these shifts, however. Some believe that sunspot cycles ultimately account for changes in atmospheric patterns of circulation, which in turn produce variations in precipitation amounts (graph 4); while others contend that variations in the composition of the atmosphere (particularly the amounts of carbon dioxide and particulate pollution) can produce similar effects. There are also those who consider the dry spells to be spontaneous and random, demonstrating no predictable cycle of recurrence.

The search for cycles necessitates the collection of data over a time span that includes several potential periods of insuf-

Soil drifts from pivot corner of irrigated wheat field despite normal precipitation during the 1975–76 winter (October–March). (Photo courtesy of the Soil Conservation Service, USDA)

ficient rainfall. Precipitation records in Nebraska are not adequate to record accurately more than four sustained droughts, however, necessitating a search for other indicators of drought which would facilitate cyclical interpretation of moisture deficiency.

Natural records—in particular, the annual growth rings of trees—may provide researchers with valuable information concerning past climatic patterns. An analysis of the tree ring chronology for Nebraska, which extends back 750 years, indicates that the area has experienced twenty-one droughts of at least 5 years' duration. One drought lasted as long as 38 years, but the average length was 12.8 years, with intervening periods averaging 23.9 years.

A periodic recurrence of drought has not been statistically demonstrated to date. Although it would serve the economic and social interests of the state to establish such a relationship (if one exists), there is abundant evidence that prolonged droughts have occurred frequently, if without regularity. This fact should be recognized in planning for the future. During the 1974 growing season, precipitation averaged 68 percent of normal throughout the state. Concurrent high temperatures with drying winds severely reduced the crop yield for the year, resulting in an estimated $1 billion loss in the value of corn, sorghum, soybeans, wheat, and hay, with an overall production deficit of 28 percent. Without millions of acres of crop land under irrigation, financial losses in Nebraska have been doubled.

Drier than normal conditions continued through 1976 with many locations reporting monthly records for minimum precipitation. Table 5 relates the rainfall during the six-month growing seasons from 1974 through 1976. For Nebraska's two largest cities, Lincoln and Omaha, 1976 was the third consecutive year with below-normal precipitation. During the driest three-year period of record, 1933–35, the total amount of moisture received by the cities was only 5.78 inches (146.8 mm.) less than in the 1974–76 period. The Nebraska Crop and Livestock Reporting Service consistently reported extremely dry topsoil and subsoil moisture conditions on farms and ranches throughout the state.

MERLIN P. LAWSON

Soil erosion by wind is not necessarily caused by drought. Continued overgrazing, particularly by horses, has caused severe wind erosion on this range in Holt County. (Photo courtesy of the Soil Conservation Service, USDA)

Table 5. Growing Season Precipitation,, 1974–76

(April through September)

Climatic Region	Normal	1974	1975	1976
Panhandle	13.80	8.96	10.54	10.85
North-Central	16.63	12.18	12.61	13.80
Northeast	19.82	14.78	17.94	12.85
Central	18.41	12.69	17.34	17.48
East-Central	21.76	15.04	17.38	13.95
Southwest	15.43	11.97	14.79	12.77
South-Central	18.92	12.11	19.35	15.06
Southeast	23.48	13.23	20.22	17.74

SOURCE: Compiled by the Conservation and Survey Division, UN–L, from data supplied by the National Weather Service.

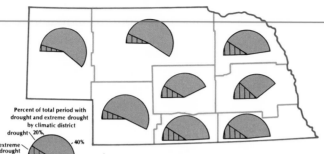

Percent of total period with
drought and extreme drought
by climatic district

Fig. 54. PERCENTAGE OF MONTHS
WITH DROUGHT, 1931–69. Analysis
of the percentage of months with
drought between 1931 and 1969 has
been conducted for each climatic district in the state. In general, the number
or percentage of months characterized
by drought decreases from west to east
across Nebraska. The largest percentage occurs in the Panhandle (60 percent) and the smallest in the East Central District (40 percent). Thus drought
existed for 40 to 60 percent of the 468
monthly records by climatic district.
Surprisingly, when the frequency of extreme drought is computed and
mapped, the distribution pattern is reversed. Although eastern Nebraska experienced fewer months with drought,
a greater percentage of its dry periods
are classified as extreme.

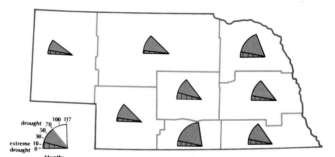

Fig. 55. MAXIMUM NUMBER OF
CONSECUTIVE MONTHS WITH
DROUGHT AND EXTREME
DROUGHT, 1931–69. Meteorologic
events such as drought are characteristically persistent in their occurrence.
This means that once dry conditions
become established, there is a tendency for them to continue. The above
map illustrates the variability of drought
persistence within the state. Although
the west experiences more months with
drought than the east, there are fewer
consecutive dry months in the western
portion of the state. Severe droughts
have been longest-lasting in the central
area of the state.

SNOWFALL

Snow is an important part of Nebraska's hydrologic cycle, both because it replenishes the soil moisture that is lost during the hot growing season and also because it protects the soil from wind erosion due to strong winter winds. Not to be overlooked is the dramatic transformation of landscape that occurs with a fresh cover of snow. With the passage of a snowstorm, the brown land and gray skies give way to a mantle of glistening white against the backdrop of a bright blue sky.

Despite these direct and indirect benefits, however, snowfalls bring social and economic problems. If we examine the entire snowfall season in Nebraska, it becomes apparent that there are two types of snowstorms, each with its own set of problems. The first type is the heavy, wet snowfall occurring at temperatures near freezing, normally in the fall or early spring. When snow occurs at temperatures close to freezing, it sticks to everything with which it comes in contact. The accumulation of this heavy, wet snow (the moisture content of snow is greatest at these temperatures) can cause tree limbs to break, especially if the trees still have their leaves, which can also accumulate snow. Electrical transmission lines as well as telephone wires collapse under the weight of this snow, leaving areas without power or communications. The loss of animal life can be quite high if cattle and calves become weighted down by the heavy snow and are prevented from reaching shelter. The impact of this type of storm may be felt for weeks because of the length of time required to repair the broken wires and replace the downed poles.

The second type of snowstorm occurs at temperatures well below freezing and normally in midwinter. Because of the lower temperatures, the snow has a much lower moisture content and is characteristically fluffy or powdery. The problem with this type of snowstorm is not its impact on communications or power transmission (powdery snow does not stick to or accumulate well on wires), but rather its impact on transportation. While heavy, wet snow can temporarily impede traffic, the transportation problem is ended once the snow is plowed to the side of the road. However, the situation is entirely different with fluffy or powdery snow, which, because of its light weight, easily becomes airborne again after accumulating on the ground. With the high winds that normally accompany midwinter snowstorms, blizzardlike conditions with near-zero visibility can result from the blowing and drifting snow. Keeping the highways open is an endless battle as snow drifts back across the highways as quickly as they are opened. The problems are not necessarily over when the storm center moves out of the region. Blowing and drifting snow may continue to hamper transportation for days after it has stopped snowing if the winds remain strong.

Fortunately, not all snowfall in Nebraska comes in the form of snowstorms. Many snowfalls last for just a few hours and bring only light accumulations. Although each snowfall season is unique in terms of the number of storms and amounts of snowfall received, there are several consistent characteristics about the state's snowfalls. The annual snowfall increases generally toward the north and west (fig. 56), averaging less than 25 inches (635 mm.) in the southeast but over 40 inches (1,016 mm.) in the northwest and north-central portions of the state. The average annual number of days with snowfall of 0.5 inch (12.7 mm.) or more exhibits the same general pattern, ranging from nine days in the south and east to fifteen days in the northwest (fig. 57).

Although the average date for the first 1-inch (25.4-mm.) snowfall varies greatly, the northwestern part of the state normally receives its first one as early as November 1, whereas the eastern portion of the state normally does not receive its first inch of snowfall until December 1, a full month later (fig. 58).

Conversely, the last snowfall of an inch or more occurs on the average around March 15 in the eastern area of the state and about April 15 in the west (fig. 59). The net result is an average snowfall season lasting from November 1 until April 15 in western Nebraska, but two months shorter, December 1 to March 15, in eastern Nebraska.

The length of time that the ground is snow-covered also varies considerably from year to year. If it is snow-covered, the most likely period is during the months of January, February, and into early March. Even though more snow is received in the northern and western areas of the state, the average depth of snow on the ground in midwinter is greatest in central and eastern Nebraska (figs. 60–63). The snow depth on January 1, for example, averages 2 inches (50.8 mm.) or more in eastern Nebraska and less than 1 inch (25.4 mm.) in the west.

KENNETH F. DEWEY

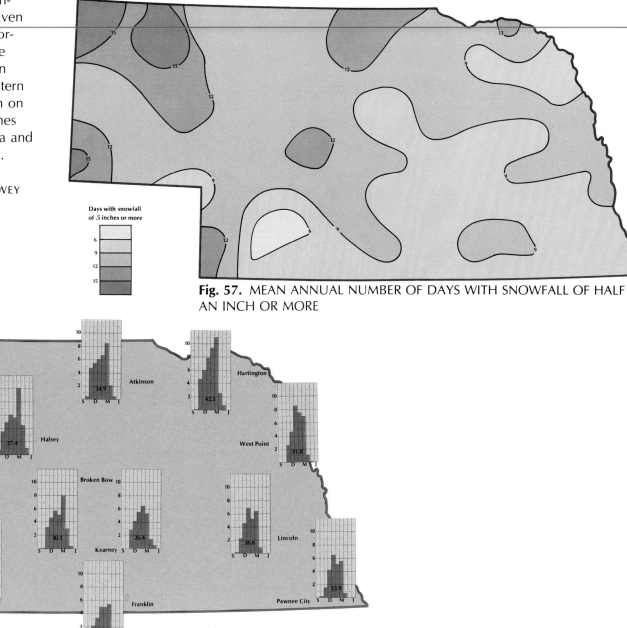

Days with snowfall of .5 inches or more

6
9
12
15

Fig. 57. MEAN ANNUAL NUMBER OF DAYS WITH SNOWFALL OF HALF AN INCH OR MORE

Fig. 56. MEAN ANNUAL SNOWFALL, 1930–60.

60

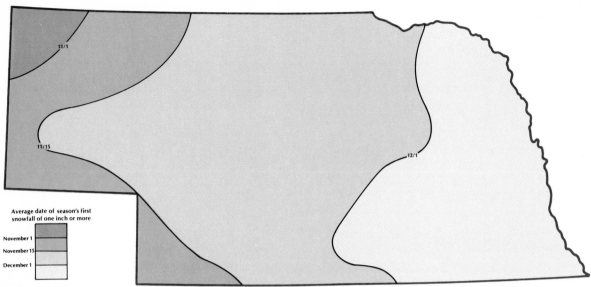

11/1

11/15

12/1

Average date of season's first snowfall of one inch or more

November 1

November 15

December 1

Fig. 58. MEAN DATE OF FIRST 1-INCH SNOWFALL

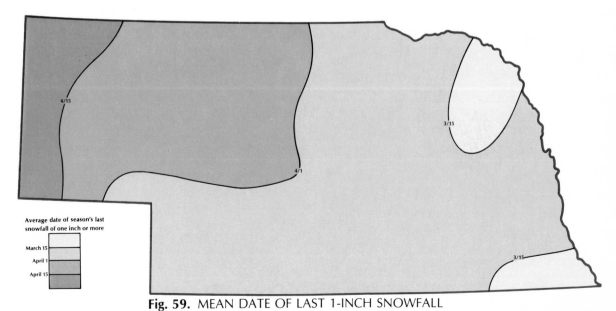

4/15

3/15

4/1

3/15

Average date of season's last snowfall of one inch or more

March 15

April 1

April 15

Fig. 59. MEAN DATE OF LAST 1-INCH SNOWFALL

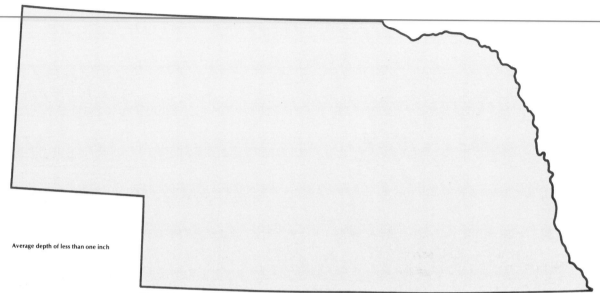

Average depth of less than one inch

Fig. 60. AVERAGE DEPTH OF SNOW, DECEMBER 1

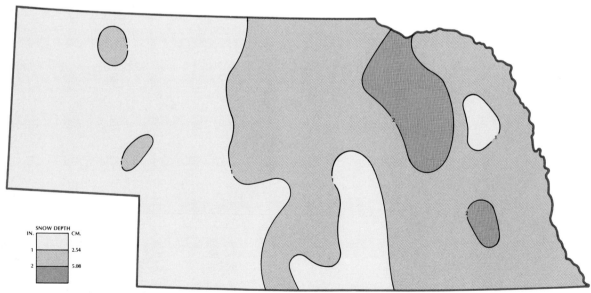

SNOW DEPTH
IN.   CM.

1   2.54
2   5.08

Fig. 61. AVERAGE DEPTH OF SNOW, JANUARY 1

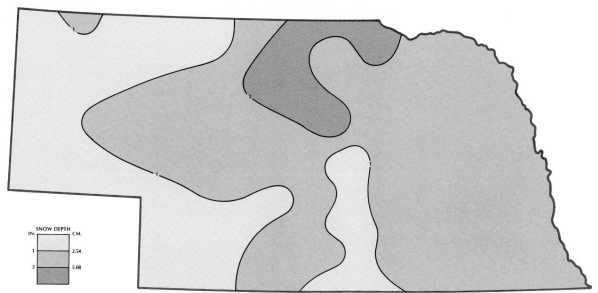

Fig. 62. AVERAGE DEPTH OF SNOW, FEBRUARY 1

SNOW DEPTH
IN. CM.
1   2.54
2   5.08

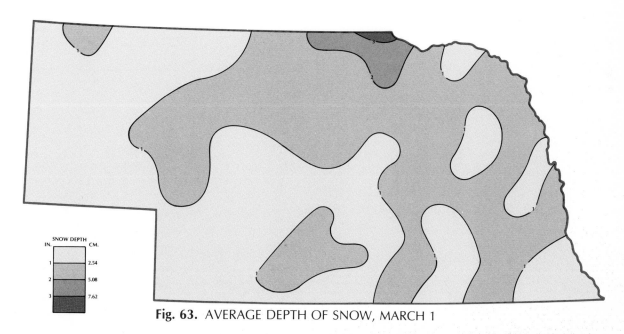

SNOW DEPTH
IN. CM.
1   2.54
2   5.08
3   7.62

Fig. 63. AVERAGE DEPTH OF SNOW, MARCH 1

BLIZZARDS

In the Great Plains region, blizzards—snowstorms with winds of thirty-five miles an hour or more and temperatures below 20° F. (−7° C.)—are the most severe type of winter storm. They endanger more persons and have accounted for more deaths in Nebraska than any other natural hazard. Stranded motorists are most often the victims of such winter storms (consider the effect when the State Civil Defense Agency estimates that 30,000 persons are traveling along Nebraska Interstate 80 at any given time).

Most blizzard deaths can be attributed to overexertion, exhaustion, or exposure. Motorists are generally advised not to leave their car if they become stuck in drifting snow or slide off the road. The swirling snow carried by high winds causes people to lose their direction easily. Rescue teams have a better chance of locating people if they remain with their cars.

Warnings are issued by the National Weather Service when the possibility of severe winter weather is forecast. Familiarity with these alerts may ensure both safety and comfort.

Cold Wave Warning. Indicates a rapid decline in temperature within twenty-four hours.

Heavy Snow Warning. Four or more inches of snow is expected within twelve hours.

Hazardous Driving Warnings. Freezing rain, drizzle, or strong winds are expected to result in extremely difficult driving conditions.

Blizzard Warning. Wind speeds of thirty-five miles per hour or more, with sufficient amounts of falling or blowing snow to lower visibility to 500 feet or less, and a temperature of 20° F. (−7° C.) or lower are expected.

Severe Blizzard Warning. Winds of forty-five miles per hour or more, with visibility near zero due to dense falling or blowing snow, and temperatures 10° F. (−12° C.) or lower are forecast.

Blizzards are common to the northern and interior United States, occurring almost annually. Severe blizzards covering large geographical areas, however, are much less frequent in occurrence. Thus, only a handful of winter storms in Nebraska can be designated as epic in proportion.

The Easter Storm of 1873

The first of these winter storms struck with unimaginable fury on Easter Sunday, April 13, 1873. Few eyewitness accounts of the unseasonable mid-April storm remain, but there is little doubt that it was one of the worst blizzards in the state's history. One account has been left by Charles Letton, a young farmer from Jefferson County who described the storm years later.

On the afternoon of Easter Sunday it began to rain and blow from the northwest. The next morning I had been awake for some time waiting for daylight when I finally realized that the dim light coming from the windows was due to the fact that they were covered with snow drifts. I could hear the noise of the wind but had no idea of the fury of the tempest until I undertook to go outside to feed the stock. As soon as I opened the door I found that the air was full of snow, driven by a tremendous gale from the north. The fury of the tempest was indescribable. The air appeared to be a mass of moving snow, and the wind howled like a pack of furies.[1]

During these early pioneering years on the plains, most of the settlers constructed sod houses or dugouts for shelter. Livestock were often stabled in primitive "barns" fashioned from forked posts partially dug into the banks of ravines with straw, prairie grass, or manure covering branches to form a fragile roof.

With great difficulty, young Letton managed to get to the ravine where his animals had been sheltered.

On looking into the ravine no stable was to be seen, only an immense snow drift which almost filled it. At the point where the door to the stable should have been, there appeared a hole in the drift where the snow was eddying. On crawling into this I found that during the night the snow had drifted in around the horses and cattle, which were tied to the manger. The animals had trampled it under their feet to such an extent that it had raised them so that in places their backs lifted the flimsy roof, and the wind carrying much of the covering away, had filled the stable

1. Charles B. Letton, "The Easter Storm of 1873," in Nebraska Society of the Daughters of the American Revolution, *Collection of Nebraska Pioneer Reminiscences* (Cedar Rapids: Torch Press, 1916), pp. 158–60.

with snow until some of them were almost and others wholly buried, except where the remains of the roof protected them.

Other accounts of the storm describe how animals were brought into the houses in an effort to keep them from perishing in the snow, wind, and cold. Many homes lost their roofs and their occupants eventually froze to death. In some instances women and children were stranded alone and forced to wait out the storm huddled in bed for warmth, or even burning furniture as their only recourse for self-preservation.

The storm lasted three days, filling east-west oriented ravines completely. Travelers who sought refuge in these breaks in the prairie soon perished, their frozen bodies not being discovered for weeks.

Mr. Letton concluded his account of the Easter storm by observing,

In the forty-six years that I have lived in Nebraska there has only been one other winter storm that measurably approached it in intensity. This was the blizzard of 1888 when several people lost their lives. At that time, however, people were living in comfort; trees, hedges, groves, stubble, and cornfields held the snow so that the drifts were insignificant in comparison. The cold was more severe but the duration of the storm was less and no such widespread suffering took place.

The Blizzard of '88

It is unrealistic to attempt to rank the severity of blizzards because their intensity varies considerably within a region as large as Nebraska. The ability of pioneers to cope with such storms during the frontier days

likewise must be taken into account when comparisons are sought. But the fabled "Blizzard of '88" has served in the minds of most Nebraskans as the historical benchmark of winter storms. Reported also as the most disastrous blizzard ever known in Montana, the Dakotas, and Minnesota, it extended also into Wyoming, Kansas, Oklahoma, and Texas. The suddenness of the storm, combined with gale winds, blowing snow, and extremely rapidly dropping temperatures resulted in the freezing to death of thousands of cattle and a severe loss of human life. Accurate records do not exist for estimating the number of people succumbing to this blizzard, but some estimates reach as high as one hundred persons.

Many accounts of the personal tragedy and suffering associated with this blizzard have been published elsewhere. One narrative of the storm, written by Dr. Paxton of Chambers, Nebraska, is included in a letter written to his wife.

I suppose you think me dead, but thank fortune I am alright. Prepare to hear of one of the closest calls that was ever my misfortune to experience. The weather here . . . has been very stormy with more snow than was ever seen here before. We have had severe blizzards every few days all winter, but on Thursday the 12th [January], there was the worst storm that was ever known in this or any other country. On the 11th, it snowed and was very blustry but on the morning of the never-to-be-forgotten 12th, the wind was blowing a soft breeze, from the south, and everyone said: "We are going to have a January thaw," but alas how untrue. In less than one minute without warning, with no indication that death and destruction would follow that awful storm, with no premonition that an im-

pending and horrible doom was awaiting them, the people were out attending to their stock, or at their respective avocations when it came. The wind blew a terrible gale, the air was full of powdered snow and so cold that hundreds of cattle and livestock of all kinds froze to death.[2]

The scene that Dr. Paxton described is typical of the drama that so many Nebraskans experienced that historic day. At 1:30 in the afternoon the doctor and three other men decided to return to their boarding house from the town store not far away.

We could not see five feet from us in any direction. We got probably within twenty feet of the house, got lost, shouted as loud as we could, but could hear nothing but threat from that fateful wind. We were not clothed to be out half an hour. After trying to find the house we started with the wind which was blowing from the northwest. We were frightful looking human beings with ice hanging from our whiskers and clothes, our faces a sheet of ice, but we staggered on. We went through corn stalks, over cultivated farms, came to trees, went in a few yards of houses, shouted and screamed, but no echoing voice returned. By this time night was approaching, but still we traveled on, determined not to yield until we were forced to do so. We finally came to some cabbage and castor bean stalks and we knew we were close to a house. We shouted long and loud and a dog heard us and barked and we followed the dog who led us to a hog shed which we welcomed with open arms. More dead than alive, we crowded in among the hogs. There was not a dry thread on us when the ice melted. My toes were frozen as

2. A copy of an extract from Dr. Paxton's letter is held by the Nebraska State Historical Society. Edited excerpts of the blizzard description are printed with their permission.

I didn't have very warm shoes and only cotton socks. I pulled my shoes off and my feet froze solid and I would have lost them only for Lou Baker, who told me to put them under his coat, I feel very grateful to him as he saved my life. He had no overshoes so he put his feet under a hog and kept them from freezing. We stayed with the hogs ten hours when the storm abated. . . . We were altogether thirteen hours in it.

These four men had wandered more than six miles from their home before they were fortunate enough to find a hog shed for refuge. Many were not as lucky and the number who died will probably never be accurately known. As Dr. Paxton concludes,

This was our experience and I wish ours had been the worse ones. Old Tom Keller was frozen to death that night. A man by the name of Glaze was found the next morning, stark and stiff within ten feet of his door. Another man was found in a door yard dead. Mrs. Crupee went out to look for her husband, who was lost in the storm, he came back in her absence and started after her, but did not find her, after getting lost and staying on the prairie all night. De Lukens, a young man, who has stayed with [us] since you left, started for his stable and has not been found. I need not go on; there were fifteen in this immediate vicinity whom I have heard of. . . . There are as many as a thousand cattle lost in this valley besides sheep, hogs and horses.

While reading the various accounts of the Blizzard of '88 one is struck with the suddenness with which the "grinding wall of snow came out of the northwest," disorienting and immobilizing all who were caught in its fury. Six decades were to pass before Nebraska would again experience a blizzard

66

of comparable magnitude. In the intervening years a modern technology would mobilize every segment of Nebraska's society against its environmental extremes. The Weather Bureau with its network of observers, sophisticated instrumentation, and electronic communications system would have been inconceivable to those who witnessed the disastrous storms of the late nineteenth century. Yet the winter of 1949 put to the test the entire arsenal of Nebraska's technical and mechanical expertise.

The "Book End" Blizzards of '49

Depending on whether you were living in western or eastern Nebraska, the blizzard of 1949 could be one of two different storms. Because of the widespread extent of the first storm, outstate Nebraskans must be given the dubious distinction of suffering through one of the worst winter blizzards in modern time. During the week of the new year, a snowfall measuring from 7 to more than 30 inches (178 to 762 mm.) was whipped by

This photo, taken after the blizzard of January 2–5, 1949, shows some of the 150 cattle that were caught on a frozen lake near Ashby, Nebraska. None of them survived. (Photo courtesy of the Nebraska State Historical Society)

forty- to seventy-mile-an-hour winds throughout much of the northern Great Basin, middle Rockies, and northwestern Great Plains. Snow drifts were cited by meteorologists as being 50 feet (15 m.) deep in places. At Chadron, in the state's western Panhandle, an average depth of 41 inches (1,041 mm.) was recorded in two days, a state record. As temperatures plummeted below zero, blowing snow produced zero visibility and roads became completely blocked, even to heavy earth-moving equipment and railroad locomotives. Newspaper accounts estimated that a total of 7,500 passengers were stranded on as many as fifty stalled trains from Illinois to Idaho.

Livestock, farms, and entire towns became isolated by the huge drifts, requiring airlift operations to provide medical supplies and food for the rural communities and endangered animals. The fact that the storm centered on the less populated western region of the state probably reduced the human loss of life to twenty. It is estimated that as many as 500,000 animals died of exposure throughout the state. Wyoming suffered livestock losses in excess of 9 million.

Cleanup operations took nearly two months with the aid of 6,000 men, 1,400 bulldozers, and 100 road graders at an estimated cost of nearly $50 million. The emotional, physical, and financial strain on northwestern and north-central Nebraska remains unsurpassed more than a quarter of a century later.

Eastern Nebraska had been spared the brunt of the storm as its path veered sharply northward into the Dakotas. Later in the month another storm belted Omaha with 13 inches (330 mm.) of snow and 50- to 60-mile-an-hour winds. Today the National Weather Service lists the January 27–28 storm as one of the city's most severe. Yet the memory of the earlier storm dwarfs it by proportion. In fact, the heavily populated eastern portion of the state remained on the fringes of the epic storms of the past hundred years. But on January 10, 1975, the area's luck ran out and the state's two largest cities, Omaha and Lincoln, virtually were stopped—cold.

The Blizzard of '75: Storm of the Century?

The weather conditions on January 9 read as if they had come out of a meteorology textbook chapter entitled "Blizzards." Two low-pressure storm centers developed to the east of the Rockies, one in southern Wyoming, the other in the Texas Panhandle. In association with the cyclonic (counterclockwise) movement of air, the southern plains were engulfed with warm, moist air from the Gulf of Mexico. To the north a polar air mass appeared to have the potential for displacing the warm air with such force as to lead forecasters in Kansas City to issue heavy snow warnings for the western two-thirds of Nebraska. Rain fell in Lincoln as the storm center deepened in northeastern Oklahoma. A winter storm watch was issued for eastern Nebraska and the heavy snow warning was canceled in the western third of the state.

By early Friday morning, January 10, the storm center had shifted northward parallel to the Kansas-Missouri state line. Snow fell over the eastern half of the state, causing travelers' warnings to be issued as the roads became packed with blowing and drifting snow. Falling barometric pressure accompanied by gusting winds and increasingly heavy snow first hit Lincoln, then Omaha. Grand Island was recording wind gusts to 42 miles an hour by mid-morning. Within minutes, a blizzard warning for Omaha and eastern Nebraska was issued. Shortly after midday, the State Patrol reported all routes into Lincoln closed. As the intensified low-pressure system moved into south-central Iowa and the cold front passed eastward out of Nebraska, snowfall began to subside but wind gusts approached 60 miles an hour. By definition, however, the storm did not become a severe blizzard until early Saturday morning when temperatures first dipped to 10° F. (−12° C.) or lower. For those out in the storm, the wind chill index hovered around 40° F. below zero (−40° C.). Fortunately for Nebraska residents, the storm moved into the Lake Superior region and Canada very rapidly. Blizzard conditions lasted less than twenty-four hours. Because the storm's predominant impact was in the eastern sector, thousands of head of livestock were spared, with only minimal losses being reported in the state. Tragically, at least fourteen persons died, in most instances from heart attacks due to overexertion.

The interest in, and obsession with, extreme weather occurrences is a characteristic which most Nebraskans and indeed most of mankind share. Our sense of adventure and intrinsic awe of nature instill in us a desire to witness floods, tornadoes, droughts, and other natural hazards. Is the true measurement of the "storm of the century" (as numerous, it would seem, as the "game of the century") such objective factors as the strength of the wind, the depth of the snow, the extremes of cold, or even the number of lives lost? If so, then our neighboring states can boast of greater calamities. Or is the measure of a natural hazard a subjective factor that can only be related to personal experience? Ultimately, the "intensity" of such a hazard can be measured only by its rather inestimable impact on each individual who has to cope with and adapt to its exigencies.

MERLIN P. LAWSON

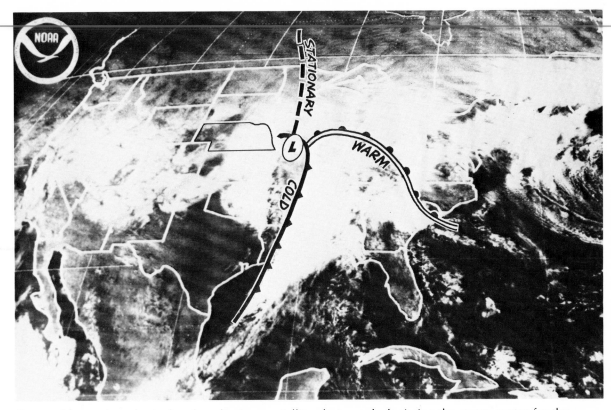

Composite weather chart of surface fronts on satellite photograph depicting the storm center for the "blizzard of '75." (Photo courtesy of NOAA, National Weather Service, with art work by Allan Tubach, *Omaha World-Herald*)

Omaha's 72d Street following the "blizzard of '75," through a telephoto lens. (Photo courtesy of the *Omaha World-Herald*)

4
WIND

Wind Speed and Prevailing Direction
Shelterbelts: Modifying Nebraska's
    Microclimate
Tornadoes: The Earth's Most Violent Winds

Wind Speed and Prevailing Direction

There are two major influences responsible for wind speed and direction across Nebraska: the topography of the region and seasonal variations in climatic controls. The state has very little surface relief. Although there is a change in elevation across the state, it is a gradual slope. With the lack of what meteorologists call surface roughness, winds can attain high velocities.

Winds in Nebraska are generally strongest in winter and early spring and lightest in midsummer. This seasonal pattern is due to the fact that the state lies in a zone of frequent mixing of warm and cold air masses. For that reason it is traversed by several well-defined low-pressure storm tracks, or paths, during winter and early spring. As a result, the average wind velocities are at a maximum during this time of year. In midsummer, however, frontal systems (caused by the displacement of warm air by cold air or vice versa) and low-pressure cells are much weaker and less frequent across the Great Plains; and except for an occasional convective thunderstorm with gusty winds, this is a period of relative atmospheric quiet and much lighter wind speeds.

There is also daily variation in wind speeds, which reach a maximum during the afternoon and are normally much lower in the early morning. The land surface is slowly heated during the day by solar radiation.

By late afternoon, rising pockets of heated air (thermals) mix with the cooler air above ground, causing turbulence and higher wind velocities. The lower atmosphere and the ground are rapidly cooling in the early morning hours, and since there is little thermal contrast, wind speeds are usually at their minimum for the day. The experienced air traveler has probably noted that early morning flights tend to be smoother than afternoon flights, which often encounter turbulence over the Great Plains.

A monsoon is commonly defined as a twice annual reversal of winds. Although Nebraska does not have a true monsoonal climate, there is a seasonal reversal in the prevailing winds. From November through April cold polar anticyclones (high-pressure, fair-weather systems) dominate the northern Great Plains, bringing a persistent flow of northerly or northwesterly winds (fig. 64). The pattern may be broken (especially at the beginning and end of the period) by warm southerly winds, but the more dominant flow quickly reestablishes itself. May is a transitional month in which incursions of cold air are replaced by incursions of warm air. By the end of May, the reversal in the prevailing wind flow has become established and the region is dominated by

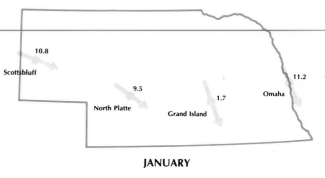

JANUARY

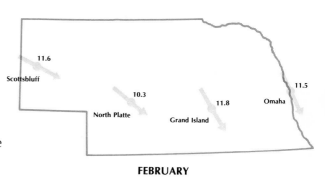

FEBRUARY

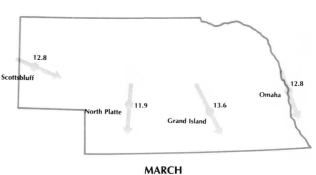

MARCH

Fig. 64. AVERAGE MONTHLY WIND SPEED AND PREVAILING DIRECTION

72

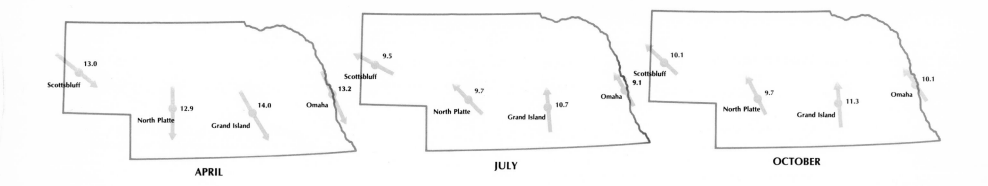

APRIL

Scottsbluff 13.0
North Platte 12.9
Grand Island 14.0
Omaha
Scottsbluff 13.2

JULY

9.5
North Platte 9.7
Grand Island 10.7
Omaha
Scottsbluff 9.1

OCTOBER

10.1
North Platte 9.7
Grand Island 11.3
Omaha
10.1

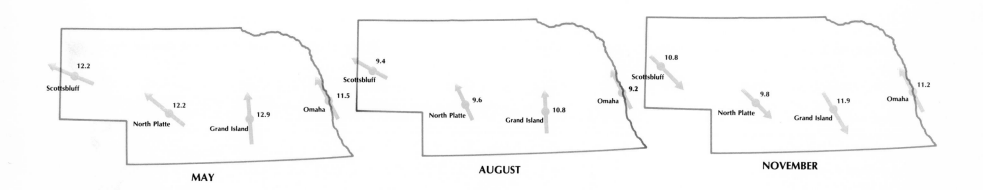

MAY

Scottsbluff 12.2
North Platte 12.2
Grand Island 12.9
Omaha
11.5

AUGUST

9.4
North Platte 9.6
Grand Island 10.8
Omaha
Scottsbluff 9.2

NOVEMBER

10.8
North Platte 9.8
Grand Island 11.9
Omaha
11.2

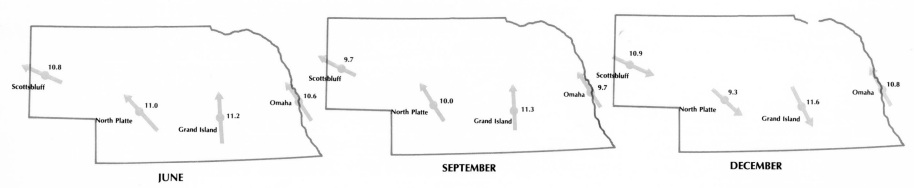

JUNE

Scottsbluff 10.8
North Platte 11.0
Grand Island 11.2
Omaha
10.6

SEPTEMBER

9.7
North Platte 10.0
Grand Island 11.3
Omaha
Scottsbluff 9.7

DECEMBER

10.9
North Platte 9.3
Grand Island 11.6
Omaha
10.8

73

southerly winds, which continue to prevail until late September. October, like May, is a transitional month. In early October the southerly flow of air dominates the state, but by the end of the month, the northerly flow has become well established over much of the region.

There are a number of practical applications for data on the prevailing wind direction and average wind speeds. For example, the design of shelterbelts must take into account the average wind conditions during the growing season. Likewise, the design of homes and offices should take into consideration the prevailing seasonal wind directions and average wind speeds in order to minimize the loss of heat in the winter and cooling in the summer.

It should also be remembered that wind is one of Nebraska's major natural resources. As many forms of energy become scarcer, wind is increasingly looked to as a source of power generation. With the present technology, storage capabilities have been designed for wind-generated power, and it is possible to envision the installation of wind generators across the state to meet growing energy needs.

KENNETH F. DEWEY

The disruption of center-pivot irrigation by trees that shelter cropland often leads, regrettably, to their removal. (Photo courtesy of the Agricultural Stabilization and Conservation Service, USDA)

SHELTERBELTS: MODIFYING NEBRASKA'S MICROCLIMATE

Evaporation results in the loss of enormous amounts of water from the soil. Historically, the construction of shelterbelts probably constituted one of the first attempts to reduce evaporative loss, which is closely related to wind speed. Windbreaks have also proved effective in controlling wind erosion and snow accumulation.

A significant reduction in wind velocity can result for a distance approaching forty times the height of the trees in the shelterbelt. With proper shelterbelt planning, a farmer can reduce wind pressure on his crops, modify soil and air temperatures, alter the precipitation pattern, and generally improve plant growth, as well as reducing evaporative loss.

Through research efforts scientists are becoming more aware of the complexity of windbreak construction and its influence on the climate just above the ground. For instance, it is now recognized that shelterbelts of the dense type planted during the drought of the thirties are not as effective as more permeable windbreaks which permit moderate penetration of wind. Specialists in applied climatology and forestry continue to search for ways to improve shelterbelt installation practices as a means of increasing their agricultural effectiveness.

MERLIN P. LAWSON

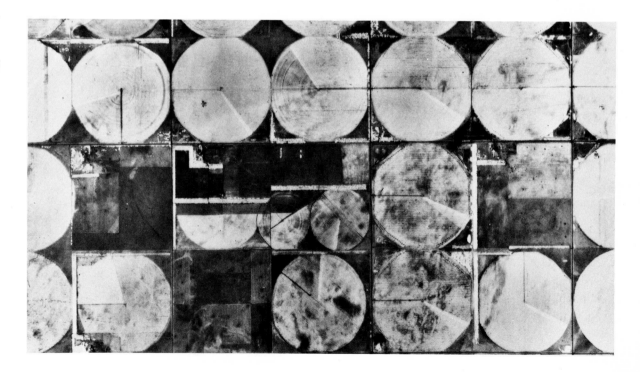

Oblique aerial view of tic-tac-toe pattern produced by shelterbelts at the University of Nebraska Field Laboratory at Mead. (Photo courtesy of the Department of Agricultural Communications, University of Nebraska–Lincoln)

TORNADOES: THE EARTH'S MOST VIOLENT WINDS

There is no wind sweeping the surface of this planet that is more violent than a tornado. Although tornadoes vary in size, intensity, length of path, and destructiveness, they possess many common characteristics that distinguish them from other storms. Tornadoes are short-lived local storms composed of revolving winds of several hundred miles per hour. The whirling vortex creates a partial vacuum which causes condensation, making the funnel cloud visible. Technically, funnel clouds become tornadoes only after extending down to the surface of the earth. Once there is contact with the ground, debris is pulled into the vortex making the funnel darker.

These funnel clouds are normally associated with severe thunderstorms. They may occur singly or in families. Often more than one funnel can be observed beneath the dark, sinister base of a thundercloud. The forward speed of tornadoes is related to that of the parent thunderstorms. For this reason, their average speed is approximately forty miles an hour.

Tornadoes usually do not extend to the ground for very long. The typical tornado path measures only a quarter of a mile wide and is seldom more than sixteen miles in length. An exception to this norm occurred, however, on May 5, 1964, when a tornado touched down near Hastings, Nebraska, traveling 70 miles northeastward to Bellwood. Miraculously, only four lives were lost as the storm narrowly missed numerous towns in its path.

Tornado funnel, consisting of condensed water droplets and dust, after leveling portions of Arcadia, Nebraska, on April 20, 1974. (Photo by state patrolman Gerald Schmitt)

The formation of tornadoes is not fully understood by atmospheric scientists, although general agreement exists that thermal and mechanical forces in combination lead to the rotary flow of a tornado vortex during particularly severe squall-line (prefrontal) thunderstorms. The most favorable area in the world for tornado formation is the Great Plains of North America, especially in spring and early summer. At that season, cold, dry air penetrates the region from Canada, often overriding maritime tropical air. The thermal imbalance causes the upward convection of air from the lower layers and the formation of large clouds. The convective triggering mechanism is most effective with the approach of a cold front toward the western edge of warm, moist tropical air from the Gulf of Mexico (fig. 65).

Tornadoes have occurred in all fifty states of the union. In recent years Nebraska has ranked fourth in tornado incidence per 10,000 square miles. During the period 1953–72 the average annual frequency of tornado sightings in the state was 34, as with approximately 650 nationally. The sea-

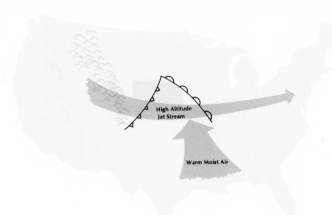

Fig. 65. CONDITIONS FAVORABLE TO TOR-
NADO FORMATION IN NEBRASKA

most prevalent between 3:00 and 7:00 p.m. local standard time. Nocturnal thunderstorms, which are common in the state, account for a surprisingly high amount of tornado activity after midnight.

Although the life span of a tornado is extremely short and its path on the average covers less than three square miles, the devastation and havoc wreaked by a tornado in seconds upon the earth is unparalleled by other natural events. The destructive action of these violent storms is caused by the combination of strong rotary winds and the sudden reduction in air pressure within the funnel. A tornado passing over a building not only rips it with winds exceeding two hundred miles per hour, but simultaneously causes it to explode outward because the air pressure inside it is greater than that inside the tornado vortex. Most tornado casualties are due to the outward collapse of buildings and the caving in of roofs.

One of the deadliest tornadoes ever to strike an American city was recorded in Omaha on Easter Sunday, March 23, 1913. Within minutes after it touched down at 5:45 p.m., at least 7,000 people were homeless, 510 were injured, and 177 were killed.

In the period 1950–73, there were forty tornado fatalities in Nebraska, half of which were related to only three separate storms in the early fifties. This averages to five deaths per 10,000 square miles, considerably less than the figure for the more heavily populated middle western and southern gulf states.

son of highest tornado incidence varies regionally, but the largest numbers are normally recorded in April, May, and June. In June, the month of highest frequency in Nebraska, the formation of tornadoes is facilitated by the northward movement of storm tracks (the favored paths for large-scale low-pressure systems and associated storms) and the increasing penetration of warm, moist air as the warm season approaches. With the dominance of tropical air during the hot summer months, there are fewer encounters between warm and overriding cold air systems and hence fewer tornadoes (graph 5).

Tornadoes have struck in Nebraska during every hour of the day, although they are

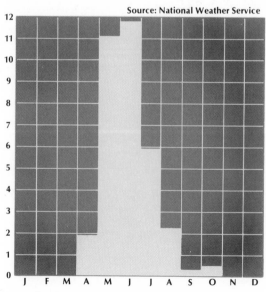

Graph 5. MONTHLY FREQUENCY OF TOR-
NADOES IN NEBRASKA, 1953–72

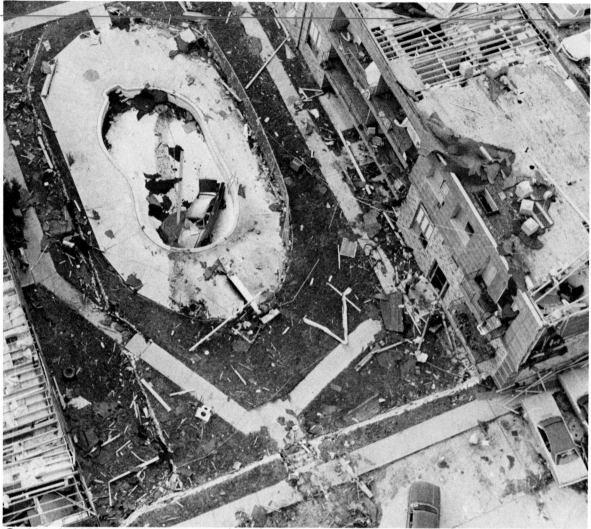

On May 6, 1975, at 4:29 p.m., a tornado with winds approaching 200 miles per hour roared into the southwest corner of Omaha, cutting a swath 600 yards wide through homes and apartments, across Interstate 80, and into crowded business and industrial areas. In twenty-nine minutes the twister destroyed or damaged more than 2,000 homes and apartments, injured about 200 people, and left three dead, a miraculously low number. Indicative of the damage, this swimming pool at an apartment complex on 84th Street was drained of water by the tornado and an auto was hurled into it. (Photo by Robert Paskach, *Omaha World-Hearld*)

There was a sharp increase in the number of reported tornadoes and a significant reduction in the number of casualties after the Weather Bureau established a tornado forecasting program in 1953. Presumably, the frequency of tornadoes did not change, but detection and warning systems were greatly improved. Today, at the National Severe Storms Forecast Center in Kansas City, Missouri, weather scientists continually strive to predict, detect, and observe potentially destructive storms across the nation. Working in conjunction with these meteorologists are people with the National Environmental Satellite Service who provide satellite photographs of developing weather systems.

Once an area has been identified as a high tornado-risk area, local offices of the National Weather Service, with the aid of Skywarn spotter networks, detect and track severe storms and tornadoes, issuing alerts as necessary. There are over five hundred local Skywarn networks comprising thousands of public-minded volunteers helping the National Weather Service to alert communities to the threat of tornadoes. These volunteers are principally rural observers, emergency personnel, and amateur radio operators. Although satellite photos and radar surveillance units can identify potential tornado-producing storms, the human eye is the only effective means of absolute identification.

Two forms of messages are used to alert the public to possible danger from tornadoes.

Fig. 66. MEAN ANNUAL TORNADO FRE-QUENCY. The annual incidence of tornadoes in Nebraska averages a little over four per 10,000 square miles. The rate varies from more than eight in the populated east to less than one in the Sandhills. Part of this difference may be due to better reporting in the more densely populated areas. A similar pattern is noticeable for heavily populated areas across the country.

Mean frequency per 10,000
square miles per year

1
2
3
4
5
6
7
8

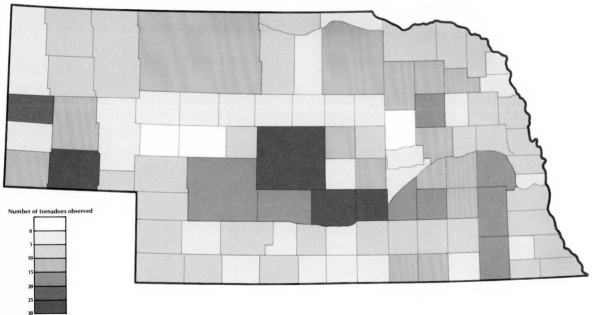

Number of tornadoes observed

0
5
10
15
20
25
30

Fig. 67. TOTAL NUMBER OF REPORTED TOR-NADOES BY COUNTY, 1950–73 (from National Severe Storms Forecast Center, National Weather Service). For the period 1950–73, all but three of the state's ninety-three counties were touched by tornadoes. County size is naturally an important factor when considering this map. In general, however, counties along the Platte River reported a larger number of tornadoes. The probability of a tornado striking a specific location in any one year is extremely small. Areas in the United States which experience the highest frequency of these storms have a chance of being struck once in 250 years. This low probability is of little comfort, however, to farmers near Petersburg, Nebraska, who lost their homes to a tornado in 1962, only to see their new replacements de-stroyed two years later.

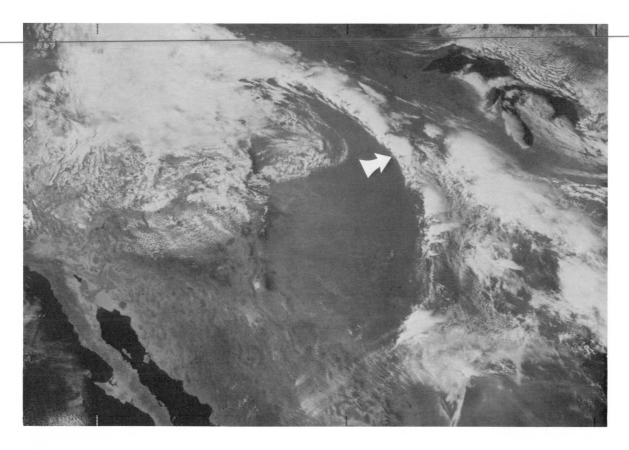

A network of weather surveillance radar units of the National Weather Service monitors severe weather conditions around the clock, seven days a week. One of these has been in operation at the local weather office in Grand Island since June 15, 1971. Its effective radius of surveillance is approximately 288 miles. (Photo by Merlin P. Lawson)

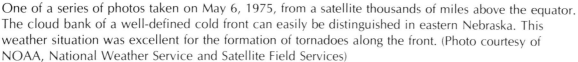

One of a series of photos taken on May 6, 1975, from a satellite thousands of miles above the equator. The cloud bank of a well-defined cold front can easily be distinguished in eastern Nebraska. This weather situation was excellent for the formation of tornadoes along the front. (Photo courtesy of NOAA, National Weather Service and Satellite Field Services)

Operating on an experimental basis are two tornado detectors which have been installed by the National Weather Service at Grand Island. The principal mechanism for detection is based on the intensity and direction of lightning discharge within a thirty-mile radius. (Photo by Merlin P. Lawson)

Tornado watches are issued by the National Severe Storms Forecast Center for areas in which severe storms, possibly with tornadoes, are likely to develop. Information concerning the area involved and the length of time covered by the watch is disseminated to local broadcasting networks, law enforcement personnel, and volunteer observers.

Tornado warnings are issued to alert persons that a tornado has actually been reported in the area. These warnings include the location and time at which the tornado was sighted, its probable course of travel, and the duration of the alert. Persons in the vicinity of the storm path should immediately initiate safety procedures.

MERLIN P. LAWSON

5
OUR CHANGING CLIMATE

Urban-Rural Contrast in Weather
  and Climate
Climatic Fluctuation

URBAN-RURAL CONTRAST IN WEATHER AND CLIMATE

As metropolitan areas expand, the physical change in landscape from vegetation to steel, cement, and asphalt is obvious. A more difficult change to document as an area becomes urbanized is the effect that the city has on the natural atmospheric processes. An increasing amount of scientific literature is being devoted to analyses of data on urban climates, almost always comparing urban data with data from nearby rural areas to show the differences between "natural" conditions and those influenced by man. These studies bear on such subjects as the effects of urban environments on human health, the design of urban structures, and climatological consequences of inadvertently altering the natural atmospheric processes.

Although we may tend to think of Nebraska as a rural state and only metropolitan areas the size of Chicago or New York City as being capable of altering the natural atmospheric environment, it has been conclusively shown that even cities with a population of only 20,000 people have a climate distinctly different from that of the surrounding countryside. Therefore, the urban-rural contrast in climate is undoubtedly a feature of Nebraska's climate and as the population of the state increases it will be-

come even more important. Moreover, the effects of several small cities like those in the more urbanized region of southeastern Nebraska are cumulative.

The concept of a rural-urban contrast in climate is illustrated in table 6, which is based on climatic data collected in many metropolitan regions. Differences in air temperature are probably the best documented. It has long been known that the center of a city is warmer than its surrounding environs. This phenomenon, called the urban heat island, occurs at night because of the contrast between surface heat retention in the city and in the surrounding countryside. Cement and asphalt lose heat by radiation at night more slowly than land covered by grass or forest. As a result, the city center may be several degrees warmer than the surrounding rural area by early morning. The actual magnitude of the urban heat island varies considerably from day to day; the temperature contrast listed in table 6 is the average for an entire year. The variation in temperature is small on stormy, windy nights but may be as large as 15° F. (8° C.) on calm, clear nights. The urban heat island has been found not only in cities like London of several million residents, but in cities as small as Corvallis, Oregon, with a population of 21,000. Of interest to the gardener is the fact that the growing season is longer in the city because of these warmer temperatures (a study of the urban climate of Washington, D.C., revealed that the average last date in spring of killing frost occurred twenty-one days later in the suburbs than in the city center).

Table 6. Comparison of Urban Climate with Climate of Surrounding Countryside

Meteorological Element	Extent of Occurrence in Urban Climate in Comparison with the Rural Environment
Solar Radiation	15 to 20% less
Temperature (Annual Mean)	.5° to 1.0° C. (1° to 2° F.) higher
Contaminants	
Condensation Nuclei and Particulates	10 times more
Gaseous Admixtures	5 to 25 times more
Wind Speed	
Annual Mean	20 to 30% lower
Extreme Gusts	10 to 20% lower
Precipitation	
Annual Total	10% more
Snowfall	5% less
Cloudiness	5 to 10% more
Fog	30% more in summer 100% more in winter
Heating Degree-Days	10% less

SOURCE: H. E. Landsberg, "Climates and Urban Planning," in *Urban Climates*, World Meteorological Organization, Technical Note No. 108 (1970), pp. 364–71.

Comparisons between city and rural wind speeds indicate that there are slower wind speeds and fewer gusts in the city. Contrary to the impression one gets when standing on a street corner with the wind funneling between two buildings, the overall effect of a city is to block the air flow and decrease the velocity of the wind.

The urban influence on precipitation is also evident when precipitation amounts for the city are compared with amounts for surrounding nonurban areas. Besides sufficient quantities of water vapor in the atmosphere, there must be condensation nuclei, or precipitation nuclei (dust particles), in the air for rain to occur, and the air mass must be lifted, causing cooling and a decreased ability to hold moisture. When the lower atmosphere passes over a metropolitan region, these natural processes are enhanced. The warm air currents rising over a city assist in forcing the air mass upward and the pollution matter acts as nuclei for condensation and raindrops. The increase in precipitation in a city may be quite large, as has been illustrated by studies of the climates of Chicago and Saint Louis.

Air pollution (caused by industrial and domestic fuel consumption) greatly reduces the amount of solar radiation reaching the ground in many metropolitan areas. Pollution emitted from industrial sources often spreads over an area in the form of a dome which can easily be seen when one approaches the city by air or automobile. As a result of air pollution, which causes a high concentration of condensation nuclei, visibilities are lower and fog occurs more frequently in a city than outside the metropolitan area. The common occurrence of smoke and fog in urban areas led to the creation of the word *smog*, a combination of *smoke* and *fog*. Despite the larger amounts of pollution, precipitation, and fog in the city, there is one significant benefit of an urban climate. Because of the higher urban temperatures and reduced wind speeds, heating requirements average about 10 percent less in metropolitan areas than in the surrounding countryside.

An examination of meteorological data for the city center of Lincoln, Nebraska, and for the airport, which is in a rural location, demonstrates the impact that an urban area can have on precipitation and temperature patterns. Precipitation and temperature data for the period 1941–70 are presented in figure 68 and table 7. The average monthly temperatures for the city were warmer than the airport temperatures for all months of the year. The maximum urban heat island, based upon monthly averages, occurred in November and December. The urban influence on precipitation is also evident. The average monthly precipitation amounts were greater at the city center location than at the airport for all months of the year. The greatest urban enhancement of precipitation occurred in June and September. Precipitation commonly occurs from convective clouds during those months, and apparently the convection is amplified by warm air rising from the city and the physical barrier of the city, which forces the air upward.

KENNETH F. DEWEY

Table 7. Monthly Temperature and Precipitation Normals for Lincoln, Downtown and Airport, 1941–70

Month	City Temp.	Airport Temp.	No. of Degrees by Which City Exceeds Airport	City Precip.	Airport Precip.	No. of Inches by Which City Exceeds Airport
January	23.1	22.2	0.9	.78	.62	.16
February	28.7	27.9	0.8	1.12	.90	.22
March	37.2	36.5	0.7	1.67	1.51	.16
April	51.9	51.3	0.6	2.67	2.51	.16
May	62.6	62.0	0.6	3.65	3.49	.16
June	72.2	72.0	0.2	5.37	4.99	.38
July	77.4	77.3	0.1	3.60	3.32	.28
August	75.9	75.6	0.3	3.45	3.27	.18
September	66.2	65.6	0.6	3.32	2.92	.40
October	55.9	54.9	1.0	1.73	1.53	.20
November	40.1	39.0	1.1	1.02	.87	.15
December	28.4	27.3	1.1	.88	.73	.15

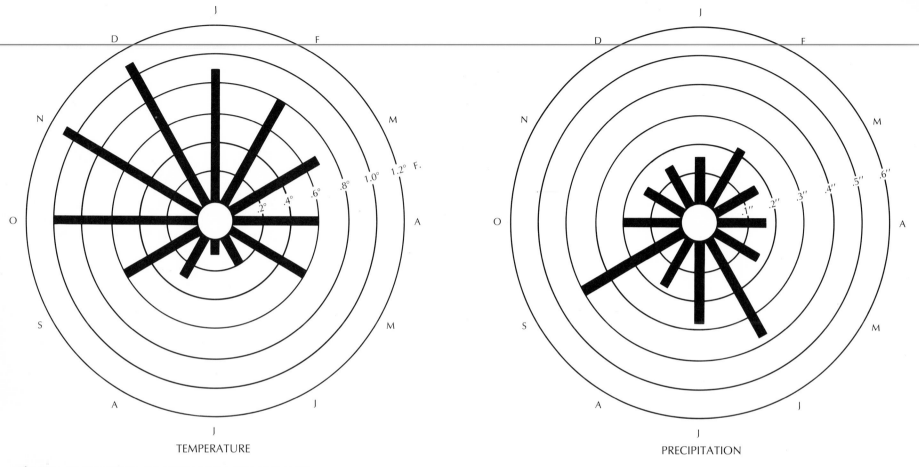

TEMPERATURE

PRECIPITATION

Fig. 68. THE EFFECT OF URBANISM ON CLIMATE

CLIMATIC FLUCTUATION

The world's climates have changed dramatically in the past and continue to change today. The present trend is one of cooling. Since the 1940s the mean global temperature has declined about .5 F. (.2 C.). The thickness and persistence of pack ice in polar waters indicate this temperature drop. Satellite weather data reveal that the area of ice and snow cover has increased rapidly in recent years, and in the Canadian Arctic, regions that were once totally free of snow in summer are now draped in white throughout the year.

A similar temperature trend has occurred in Nebraska in recent years. It appears that winters and summers are becoming cooler while the transitional seasons of autumn and spring are remaining about the same. A pronounced warming trend began close to the turn of the century, peaking in 1940. Even the armadillo was able to extend its range northward into Nebraska by that date. With the current reversal in temperatures, the armadillo is again retreating to the south.

Climatologists are becoming increasingly concerned about the continued global decline in temperature, for they recognize that substantial environmental disruption can ensue from seemingly minor fluctuations in climatic patterns. A noticeable deviation in the general circulation of the atmosphere is associated with global cooling and often leads to changes in precipitation patterns. Thus in recent years the expansion of polar winds has blocked moisture-bearing equatorial winds from bringing rainfall to the sun-parched Sahel of Africa, Central America, the Middle East, and India.

For Nebraskans, the current cooling trend may mean shorter growing seasons with more summer precipitation. Scientists from the Universities of Nebraska and Wisconsin have independently documented climatological changes in Nebraska from the early nineteenth century to the modern "normal" period. Lower temperatures generally have been accompanied by an increase of 20–30 percent in summer precipitation on the plains.

Long-range weather forecasters are not certain whether the present apparent climatic shift will continue, because they do not fully understand the causes of climatic change. The changing weather is apparently related to differences in the amount, type, or distribution of energy received at the earth's surface from the sun. Some weather scientists have tried to relate sunspot activity to changing climate patterns. Others look to astronomical relationships such as the vari-

"Should we get ready for the next ice age?" (By Einar, courtesy of the *Lincoln Star*)

able distance of the earth from the sun, the tilt of the earth's rotational axis, or the date when the earth is nearest the solar cloud.

There is growing concern among researchers that man's pollution of the atmosphere accounts for the present cooling trend. Although large amounts of carbon dioxide (CO_2) are released by burning fossil fuels and it is thought that CO_2 absorbs

terrestrial radiation, the polluted atmosphere reflects, absorbs, or scatters incoming solar radiation.

An increasing number of oceanographers, however, believe that it is the oceans rather than the atmosphere which will first reveal future climatic conditions. For instance, these researchers have linked weather patterns over the United States to variations in sea-surface temperatures in the Pacific. Areas of ocean as large as 1 million square kilometers (386,138 square miles) appear to exhibit unusually warm or cold temperatures for perhaps several years in succession. Colder than normal winters in the western United States and warmer than usual winters in the east are associated with abnormally warm water in the mid-Pacific. The tendency for oceanic changes to occur relatively slowly leads to optimism about the possibility of long-range weather forecasting.

Regardless of the cause or predictability of climatic change, meteorologists recognize that even a one percent decrease in the amount of sunlight reaching the earth's surface could disrupt the delicately balanced global weather system enough to bring about another ice age. The present climate is anomalous within recent geological time. At least seven episodes of glaciation have taken place in less than the last million years, and world temperatures have reached present levels only about 5 percent of that time. Atmospheric circulation patterns characteristic of ice age climates may take only a century or two to develop. Unfortunately, it is impossible to state now whether the current cooling trend is the end of the present interglacial period or simply a random fluctuation from some long-term "normal."

MERLIN P. LAWSON

APPENDIX
State and Federal
Climatological Publications

One of the programs of the National Weather Service is the publication of climatic data in a form that permits broad application for solving problems or understanding the climatic environment. The publications likely to be in greatest demand are briefly described below; a more comprehensive review of federal climatological publications is presented in *Selective Guide to Published Climatic Data Sources*, Key to Meteorological Records Documentation No. 4.11. This booklet can be obtained for one dollar from the Superintendent of Documents, U.S. Government Printing Office, Washington, D.C. 20402.

Climatological Data. This publication presents basic climatological data in its monthly and annual issues for each state (or combination of states). The monthly issue contains a locator map and station listing. Daily measurements and monthly summaries of precipitation and temperature are included. In addition, each issue contains data on wind, relative humidity, snowfall, snow on the ground, evaporation, and daily soil temperature for stations which collect such data. Monthly and seasonal snowfall, and monthly and seasonal heating degree-days are summarized in the July issue only. When unusual weather has occurred within the state during the month, a narrative description of it is included.

The annual issue of *Climatological Data* presents monthly and annual averages and departures from long-term averages of temperature and precipitation. Also tabulated are temperature extremes and freeze data, monthly and annual average and extreme soil temperatures at selected depths, water available in the soil to plants, precipitation, and precipitation deficiencies. A station index table and locator map are given for the convenience of the user.

Climatological Data, National Summary. This publication contains selected climatological data for each month and annually at selected stations across the United States. It presents narrative descriptions of general weather conditions as well as river and flood information. Tabulated statistics are given for temperature and precipitation extremes, heating degree-days, rawinsonde data for standard pressure surfaces, solar radiation, ozone, snowfall, percentage of possible sunshine, and tracks of cyclones and anticyclones. Upper air winds, surface wind roses and heights of constant pressure surfaces are also summarized for selected stations.

The annual issue includes similar data summaries as well as descriptions of weather phenomena of particular interest such as tornado paths, river and flood conditions, and hurricane tracks.

Local Climatological Data. This publication is issued monthly for approximately three hundred cities and towns in the United States which maintain National Weather Service stations. There are currently seven of these observation stations in Nebraska: at Grand Island, Lincoln, Norfolk, North Platte, Omaha, Scottsbluff, and Valentine. The tabulation consists of daily information on temperature, heating degree-days, dew point, precipitation, snowfall, pressure, wind, sunshine, and sky cover.

Local Climatological Data Annual Summary with Comparative Data. This publication is the annual equivalent of the monthly publication described above. It contains a table of basic climatological data for the current year: average monthly and annual temperature, precipitation (including snowfall), and heating degree-days. Information concerning station history and instrument exposure is also provided.

Hourly Precipitation Data. Available for each state (or combination of states), the monthly issues present daily and hourly precipitation data from stations equipped with automatic recording gauges. The annual issue contains monthly and annual totals of precipitation, together with a station index.

Weekly Weather and Crop Bulletin. Especially valuable to agriculturists, this weekly periodical briefly summarizes the weather and its effect on crops and farm activities over the entire United States and adjoining areas as feasible. It is distributed from Washington, D.C., about noon each Tuesday. A narrative summary of the weather of the week is presented with respect to crops. The current condition of small grains, corn, soybeans, cotton, other crops, pastures, and livestock is discussed. Moisture characteristics are mapped during the growing season. Heating degree-days are calculated for the months of October through March. During the spring, a summary of ice conditions of the Great Lakes is also featured. Of significance to Nebraskans, drought persistence is mapped during periods of insufficient moisture for crops or pasture.

Nebraska Weekly Weather and Crop Report. Published in cooperation with the National Weather Service and Statistical Reporting Service, U.S. Department of Agriculture, this fact sheet presents a brief account of the previous week's weather, crop conditions, livestock concerns, and other items of agroclimatic importance. A precipitation map for each week, compiled from selected stations, is included. This weekly publication is available from the U.S. Department of Agriculture, Lincoln, Nebraska 68501.

Preliminary Climatic Summary for Nebraska. The Conservation and Survey Division of the University of Nebraska–Lincoln tabulates monthly temperature and precipitation data for selected stations throughout the state. A brief narrative accompanies tables of temperature extremes, precipitation, and departure from normal precipitation. Precipitation is also mapped for selected stations as well as each of eight climatic divisions (regions) of the state.

MERLIN P. LAWSON

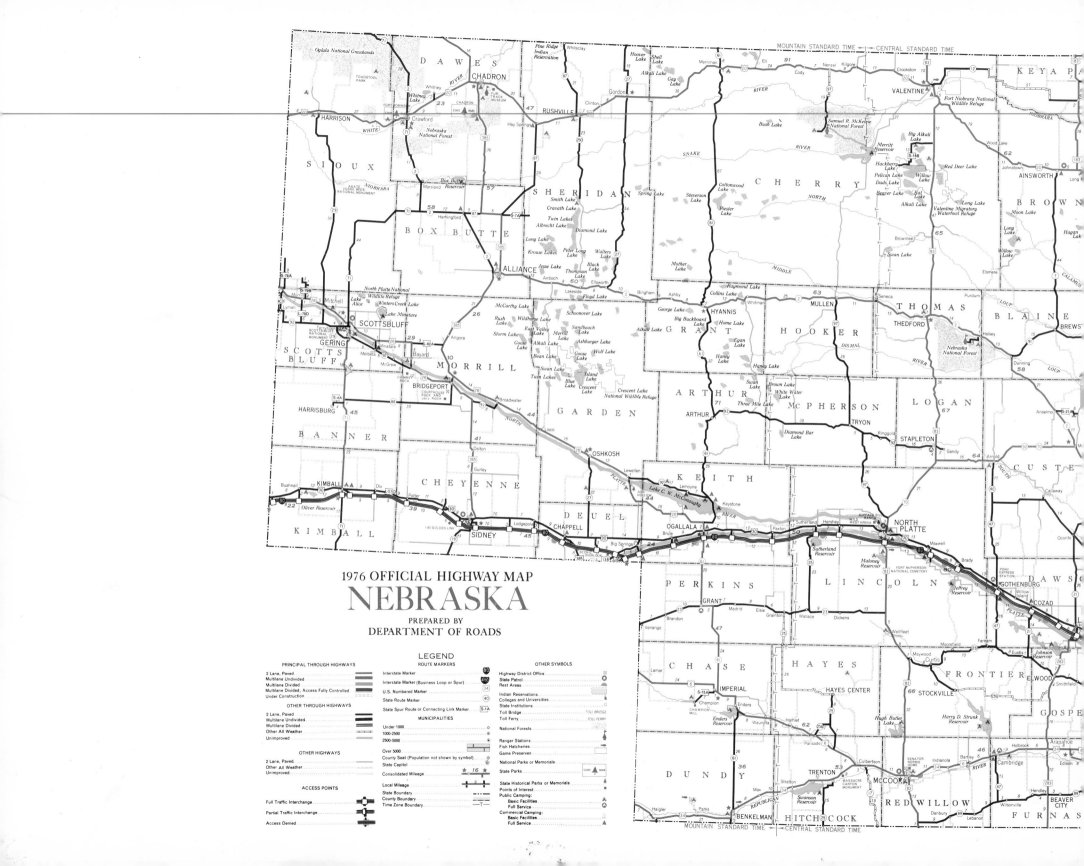

1976 OFFICIAL HIGHWAY MAP
NEBRASKA

PREPARED BY
DEPARTMENT OF ROADS

LEGEND

PRINCIPAL THROUGH HIGHWAYS

ROUTE MARKERS

OTHER SYMBOLS

PRINCIPAL THROUGH HIGHWAYS

2 Lane, Paved
Multilane Undivided
Multilane Divided
Multilane Divided, Access Fully Controlled
Under Construction

OTHER THROUGH HIGHWAYS

2 Lane, Paved
Multilane Undivided
Multilane Divided
Other All Weather
Unimproved

OTHER HIGHWAYS

2 Lane, Paved
Other All Weather
Unimproved

ACCESS POINTS

Full Traffic Interchange
Partial Traffic Interchange
Access Denied

ROUTE MARKERS

Interstate Marker
Interstate Marker (Business Loop or Spur)
U.S. Numbered Marker
State Route Marker
State Spur Route or Connecting Link Marker

MUNICIPALITIES

Under 1000
1000-2500
2500-5000
Over 5000
County Seat (Population not shown by symbol)
State Capitol
Consolidated Mileage
Local Mileage
State Boundary
County Boundary
Time Zone Boundary

OTHER SYMBOLS

Highway District Office
State Patrol
Rest Areas
Indian Reservations
Colleges and Universities
State Institutions
Toll Bridge
Toll Ferry
National Forests
Ranger Stations
Fish Hatcheries
Game Preserves
National Parks or Memorials
State Parks
State Historical Parks or Memorials
Points of Interest
Public Camping:
    Basic Facilities
    Full Service
Commercial Camping:
    Basic Facilities
    Full Service